THE LIFE ANI

MARY WEBSTER

THE LIFE AND MINISTRY OF
MARY WEBSTER

A WITNESS IN THE EVANGELISTIC
MINISTRY OF E. STANLEY JONES

Compiled & Edited by
ANNE MATHEWS-YOUNES

THE LIFE AND MINISTRY OF MARY WEBSTER:
A WITNESS IN THE EVANGELISTIC MINISTRY OF E. STANLEY JONES
Compiled and Edited By Anne Mathews-Younes

Copyright © 2017 by The E. Stanley Jones Foundation

Published By
The E. Stanley Jones Foundation
Email: anne@estanleyjonesfoundation.com
Website: www.estanleyjonesfoundation.com

Cover and Interior Design By
Shivraj K. Mahendra

ISBN-13: 978-1544191799
ISBN-10: 1544191790

MADE IN USA

DEDICATION

*This book is dedicated to
the World Wide Christian Ashram Movement
founded by E. Stanley Jones in 1930, and to all who wish
to be a part of this Christ-centered adventure
in Kingdom of God living!*

CONTENTS

PREFACE

by Claude Webster

WHEN MY MOM FIRST HEARD Brother Stanley speak I was 5 years old. That moment in time set about a cascade of lifelong events for her and for our family.

When I was about 8 years old, I remember Brother Stanley coming to our farm to visit us. I was so impressed with him and he made a mark on my heart that I carry with me to this day, all because the call of God fell upon my mom. I was struck by the way he dressed, the way he carried himself and even by the way he ate his fruit. The stories he shared with me about hunting man-eating tigers in India and seeing his well-traveled aluminum suitcase drew my spirit to him. He loved to tell stories of India and his ministry. He also loved the country breakfast that my mom would cook for him. I could tell he loved the Lord and every chance I got I asked him to have a word of prayer with me.

God used Brother Stanley in so many ways to influence my life and my mom's life. I am sure he was instrumental in blessing many others as well. One day when I was older, we invited him to go swimming with us at the public pool in Kewanee, Illinois. While we were swimming, I asked him to baptize me and he complied. What an honor it was for me to be baptized by such an awesome man of God. It was a special spiritual moment in my life!

My mother traveled a lot both nationally and internationally with Brother Stanley and other Ashram leaders. I knew that God was using her for His purpose and she displayed her deep commitment to be His instrument. While she traveled, my father's sister Aunt May, who lived with us, took care of my brother and me. Aunt May had been crippled, when in 1950, our family car was hit head on by a truck driver who was passing on a hill. That accident had taken my dad's life. Aunt May loved us as her own children and I cared for her and loved her deeply.

When I married in 1967, Brother Stanley gave a beautiful gift to my wife whom he had never met. I am sure my mom had told him about her. His giving and loving heart touched both of us. No one really knew about that expression of love toward Jan and me, except us and my mom. I know the Lord was smiling.

Today, I have a heart for missions because of my mother and Brother Stanley. The mission trips that I have experienced enriches my love to serve. My mom and Brother Stanley were responsible for instilling in me the need to spread the gospel. I am so blessed to have known them both.

Brother Stanley would often say, "Where He leads me I will follow. What He feeds me I will swallow!" I know that it takes commitment and love to follow that guidance. My mom was a picky eater and so am I. On a recent trip to Nicaragua that saying resounded in my ears at every meal of rice and beans and other spicy dishes. I smiled to myself and remembered Brother Stanley's advice and followed it! I also taught the children at the mission in Pueblo Nuevo to hold up three fingers and affirm that "Jesus is Lord."

I miss my mom and Brother Stanley so much. Their dedication to Jesus gives me energy to face each new day. I love them for that and for so much more.

CLAUDE WEBSTER
Retired Chief Pilot at The Iowa Farm Bureau,
West Des Moines, Iowa
Substitute teacher at Adult Bible Fellowship,
Capitol City Church, Des Moines, Iowa

FOREWORD

by Roberto Escamilla

I KNEW MARY WEBSTER for a period of several years while she was part of the Christian Ashram's Evangelist Missionary Team. It was my privilege to be one of the speakers along with her in several Ashrams. Obviously, I heard her share her message often and always with a glad and grateful heart.

Brother Stanley invited her to be an Ashram speaker because she incarnated the Ashram principles and lived the Christian faith on a daily basis. Mary was able to internalize the Ashram spirit especially when it came to the concept of "loving" persons as they are. That was her primary message.

Mary had a radiant personality. Her smile was contagious and indeed sincere. On one occasion, I remember Brother Stanley, in referring to Mary's radiant face, that she appeared, "to have swallowed a light bulb." She surely radiated light.

Her sermons, or I prefer to call them "messages" or "religious talks" were practical and down-to-earth presentations that reached the hearts of men and women, not only in this country, but around the world. She identified with people of other cultures, languages, and religions and generously devoted her time to get to know them.

I am grateful to Anne Mathews-Younes for her incredible and careful research and her excellent editorial skills in the preparation of this marvelous collection of messages from Mary Webster. They will inspire and encourage present and future generations to walk forward and look upwards and not be afraid.

Jesus is Lord!

BRO. ROBERTO ESCAMILLA
One of "The Four" and
Interim President,
United Christian Ashrams International

INTRODUCTION

BY ANNE MATHEWS-YOUNES

JONES WAS CONVINCED that the revitalization of the
Christian church was going to come through the laity. He
pointed out, for example, that Jesus was a layman and it
was a group of scattered non-Apostolic Christians who
founded the church at Antioch. However, according to
Jones, in the third century that laity was pushed to the
edges of the church, and the clergy became the focus and
central decision makers. Jones comments on this history,
recorded in Acts 6:4, of the relegation of the laity to the
edges of Christianity.

I have the feeling that the disciples made a blunder
when they said, "We will give ourselves to prayer

15

and the ministry of word. And we'll turn over this other work, that is the serving of tables to the lay people." Now, that may seem to be a very spiritual step. The apostles would give themselves to prayer and to the ministry of the word and turn over to the lay people the management of the material side of things. Personally I have come to the conclusion that they missed their step. At this point, they drove a wedge into life between the material and the spiritual. The spiritual was up here and the material was down here. The apostles would give themselves to the spiritual and another group, a lay group, would give itself to the material. I believe that it drove a disastrous wedge into life between the sacred and the secular, between the spiritual and the material.[1]

However in spite of this early bifurcation of the material and the spiritual, the laity emerged as an early center of spiritual power. Jones continues,

An interesting thing happened when the apostles separated the seven (the laity) to attend to the material rather than the spiritual. Those seven laypersons actually become the center of spiritual power. The initial revival in Christianity breaks out through them. First it was Stephen who precipitated a revival in Jerusalem and paid for it with his own martyrdom. Then Philip, taking up the banner from the fallen Stephen, went down to Samaria and a

[1] Anne Mathews-Younes, *Living Upon the Way*, p. 285.

great revival broke out. Then the apostle Philip sits down with Peter and John to learn what was happening with these revivals and in an effort to regularize what the Disciples couldn't produce. So it was this lay group that first preached the gospel outside of Jerusalem and into Samaria and to the utmost parts of the earth. The spiritual initiative (to share the Gospel) seemed to be taken on by this lay group in part because apparently they were keeping life together as a unit, (i.e., the material and the spiritual) whereas the Disciples were separating it.

Two things are important to note. In the beginning we see that the laity promulgated Christianity. I believe that we have got to get back to the idea that the center of gravity in the Christian church is not the pulpit; it's the pew. If the church is pastor-centered then the output will be rhetoric, if it is lay-centered, the output will be action. It will be the Word become Flesh, not the word become word.[2]

Jones believed that we must have a strong and energetic lay movement within Christianity and that the church must remedy these past blunders and re-engage the laity. Jones quotes the famous historian and theologian Harnack[3] who said, "All the early "conquests" (of the

---

[2] Jones, *Christ at the Round Table*, p. 109.

[3] Adolf Van Harnack (1851–1930), German theologian and church historian who was very interested in practical Christianity and not merely theological systems.

Church) were carried out through laymen." A lay group in Antioch was on fire with the love of God. According to Jones, we must get that energy back into our churches through lay evangelism.

The story of Mary Webster is an illustration of the power of a laywoman to become a center of evangelistic and spiritual power. Jones met Mary Webster in the 1950s and found her to be a profound example of how an ordinary life transformed and redeemed could become a force for sharing the love of Jesus Christ to everyone she encountered.

> Mary feels that she is not the source of things but only the channel and that God speaks to her directly. And He does! She says: "A watch doesn't create time, it simply registers it. A violin doesn't create music, it simply registers the music in the violinist. So we don't create, we transmit." She is the clearest channel of transmission I've ever seen.[4]

Jones always included lay witnesses in the Christian Ashrams for he wanted everyone to know the "how" of living a life following Christ. People may be more or less convinced that Christianity is true, but how to you get it?

Mary Webster knew how to answer that "how" question. Let me share an illustration.

> One evening Mary was sitting in the dining car of a train. It was late and she could not find a place to sit in the coach, so she went to the dining car. She

---

[4] E. Stanley Jones, *Growing Spiritually*, p. 218.

sat down next to a man who offered her a cigarette. She said, "No thank you, I don't need it."

He offered her a drink. Again she said, "No thank you, I don't need it." He responded, "What do you mean, you don't need it?" "Well," she said, "I don't need it, I have something better." He asked her, "Where have you been?" She responded, "Chicago." "What were you doing there?" "Speaking." "On what?" "On Religion." And with that he and his seatmates covered their glasses. She said, "You need not do that. It (alcohol) has nothing to do with what I am talking about." "All right" they said, "go ahead and talk to us about what you have." And she began and the whole dining car was gathered around her listening, including the waiter and no one ordered a drink. One man said to her, "Where did you get this?" She replied, "At the foot of the cross." "How did you get to the foot of the cross?" "At the end of my rope." For two and one half hours, they listened to this young woman describe the "how" of Christianity. That is what people really want to know.

Mary was a life long learner who was eager to take what she learned through following Christ and to risk her all to be Christ's witness. One day, she said to Jones,

"Brother Stanley in the name of Jesus, please expect bigger things of me, and help me to surpass your expectations. I'm not asking for flattery. I'm begging you to take me out to that point of no return, out of the safety zone to where nothing is predictable. There are big things to be done in this world that won't wait forever so that's why I ask you to dream up the greatest possible thing you can think of that a woman can do and share your dream with me, and then hand me the pick and shovel and tell me to go to work." Jones commented, "Wouldn't pastors like that, if church members would make that kind of an offer to them."

Mary was also open to feedback and criticism. She once asked an Ashram friend, if he would be honest and kind enough to point out her weaknesses so she could grow.

"You should have seen the look on his face. It was precious. He wanted to say something to me, but he was afraid of offending me so I told him he would do me a favor, and so bless his heart he said, "Well, if you would suffer a suggestion, it is your voice. It has a tenseness in it that isn't in your character. It is too high and if you would try pitching it lower and speaking more slowly, you would be easy to listen to." The poor man looked as if he had done one of the hardest things he'd been called upon to do for the Lord. "As you know Brother Stanley, I never admired anyone more than I did him, for it takes a lot of courage and deep compassion for a person to risk disfavor by telling them something that might offend them. I told him I knew he must like me a lot to be willing to help me. I added that I wouldn't tell anyone about our discussion but if when we next saw each other and if I had made any improvement we would laugh and rejoice about it together.

Mary went right to work on her voice!

Now to some personal memories of Mary Webster. I met her when I was 12 years old and attending a Christian Ashram with my grandfather, E. Stanley Jones. What struck me at that young age was her engaging and almost unbelievable life story but more so her exuding love as she engaged with the younger members of the Ashram community. Her love was palpable and offered with no restraint. I had never met such a person.

Some years later, I traveled in India with my grandfather and Mary where she was a most delightful traveling companion. I frequently witnessed her speak with other laymen and laywomen and her down to earth presentation of Jesus captivated all who listened to her.

Mary carefully attended to my grandfather when he was hospitalized in 1971 after a stroke and was later his able secretary as she helped transcribe his last book, *The Divine Yes*. She remained in touch with our family over the years and her death in 2004 was a personal loss to me, but not a tragic one, for I knew that she would see Jesus!

This book first introduces the reader to Mary Webster through a "constructed" conversation between Mary and Brother Stanley using Mary's unpublished autobiography interspersed with Jones' writing about Mary from his book, *Growing Spiritually*. Following, there are six original talks by Mary Webster, delivered at a Christian Ashram in the 1960s and which were faithfully transcribed from audiotapes given to me by the Rev. Dr. Jerry Wortham.

21

These talks tell Mary's story as well as her experience with the Holy Spirit, and her role as a witness in love to the transforming power of Jesus Christ. You will note her transparency as she shares the story "straight" and hides none of her brokenness or challenges as she follows Jesus. Her personal relationship with Christ and her openness to his guidance is illustrated in each of these talks.[5] The concluding sermon (p. 247) is one that E. Stanley Jones preached in the late 1950s about his view of the influence of Mary Webster as a powerful lay witness.

Mary Webster's life surely illustrates the authority of a laywoman to preach the gospel and to witness to our risen Lord.

The E. Stanley Jones Foundation is grateful to our many friends and supporters who have contributed to re-introducing the ministry of E. Stanley Jones, and now Mary Webster, to a new generation of readers. Special gratitude to Katherine Krause who suggested using Mary's life as a reflection piece for others and to Shivraj Mahendra whose theological gifts, publishing skills and friendship made this book possible.

---

[5] The reader may find some "duplicate" passages and illustra-tions among these talks by Mary Webster. In an effort to be faithful to her spoken words, the editor has elected to offer them as delivered without removing duplicative materials.

Mary Webster in 1959

Mary Webster in 1960s

2

THE LIFE

OF

MARY WEBSTER

MARY ELLA MACPHERSON was born in Peoria, Illinois, August 4, 1917. As an infant, she lived in Cedar Rapids, Iowa until the death of her mother in the sinking of the *Columbia Excursion* steamship on the Illinois River on July 5, 1918. Mary, who at that time was a toddler, went to live with her mother's relatives in Peoria, Illinois because her father worked for the railroad and was not often home.

Mary married Roy Webster on February 22, 1945 and had two sons Ted and Claude. Roy tragically died in a car accident on August 11, 1951. Mary later married Hugh Tattersall who predeceased her. Mary Webster Tattersall died in Des Moines, Iowa on August 25, 2004.

Mary Webster served as a lay colleague of E. Stanley Jones and worked with him in Christian Ashrams in North

America and internationally beginning in the 1950s until Jones' death. She accompanied him on his last evangelistic trip to Japan in 1971 and helped transcribe Jones' final book *The Divine Yes* which was published after Jones' death in 1973.

Mary is survived by her son Claude Webster and several grandchildren and great-grandchildren.

Mary Webster and Claude Webster, c.1998

Mary Webster in 1990s

Mary Webster and E. Stanley Jones, c. 1960s

3

A "Conversation"
Between E. Stanley Jones
and Mary Webster

E. STANLEY JONES believed that the revitalization of the church would come through the laity and he consistently highlighted their significant contributions. Jones wrote, "If the church is pastor-centered then the output will be rhetoric, if it is lay-centered, the output will be action. It will be the Word become Flesh, not the word become word." (Jones, *Christ at the Round Table*, 109).

Jones always included lay witnesses in the Christian Ashrams for he wanted everyone to know the "how" of living a life following Christ. He believed that we could each be transformed as we surrendered our lives to Jesus and could then draw on the power of the Holy Spirit as we moved through our lives.

Jones met Mary Webster in the 1950s and found her to be a profound example of how an ordinary life transformed and redeemed, could become a force for sharing the love of Jesus Christ to all she encountered.

This "conversation" is constructed using Mary's unpublished autobiography interspersed with Jones' writing about Mary Webster drawn from his book, *Growing Spiritually.* This constructed "conversation" was possible thanks to Mary's son, Claude Webster who graciously shared Mary's words from that unpublished autobiography. I am also grateful to Abingdon Press which permitted me to draw on the material about Mary Webster from Jones' *Growing Spiritually.*[1]

- Editor

---

[1] E. Stanley Jones, *Growing Spiritually* (Nashville, TN: Abingdon-Cokesbury, 1953).

INTRODUCTION

by E. Stanley Jones

THE VERY CENTER of the Christian faith is the Incarnation, in which the Divine Word becomes flesh -the Idea becomes Fact. All other faiths are the word become word, the idea projected as an idea. In Jesus the Idea walked. It spoke in human life and manifested itself in human relationships. Jesus transformed religion from idealism to realism.

Where this Christian faith is sincerely tried, it becomes incarnate as fact. It works in human relationships. And wherever it is tried, it produces something so exquisitely beautiful that we stand "lost in wonder, love, and praise."

From many outstanding examples of Christian growth I am picking one and for several reasons. One is that the person is an ordinary person, with ordinary education, and with ordinary abilities. The second is that she was placed in a very commonplace situation -on a farm. And third, she wasn't always what she is now. And because she was average, I pick her out to let the average person see what can happen when average life is fully surrendered to God and responsive to His will. And I pick her out because in doing so I can easily look past her and beyond her and above her to the source of her life and power - Christ. One can so easily see that attached to Christ, she has everything, and apart from Him she has little. I wrote to her one day: "Sister Mary, I hope all this attention and adulation you are getting will not go to your head, but take you to your knees." She wrote back: "Brother Stanley, it doesn't go to my head, it just hasn't got my name on it. It doesn't belong to me at all. So I lay it all at His feet as fast as it comes."

MARY WEBSTER:

"It started in a very unpromising way...."

Most people celebrate Christmas on December 25th. So did I, until March 19, 1950 when Christmas became very personal to me! An announcement was made at my church that a very famous missionary from India, a Dr. E. Stanley Jones, would be speaking 35 miles from my home. At the word "India," I was instantly interested but I had never heard of the missionary, E. Stanley Jones. However, in school I had read "Kim" by Rudyard Kipling, and had become fascinated with the magic of India, and I hoped that the speaker would show us ropes coming out of bottles, slight-of-hand tricks and share artifacts from India. My only reason for going was to be "entertained!"

Sitting in a church doesn't make you a Christian, any more than sitting in a hen house makes you a chicken!

I sat in the front row, in case he showed slides. However, the evangelist did not "entertain" us, rather he explained God's "Plan of Salvation." I felt safe! I had 13 jobs in my small country church! However he unnerved me when he said:"Sitting in a church doesn't make you a

33

Christian, any more than sitting in a hen house makes you a chicken!""You have to be born again! If you dropped your watch in the road and a car ran over it, you wouldn't pick up the broken pieces and take it to a jeweler and ask him to fix it! The jeweler would look at you in amazement and tell you that you needed a new watch! If we bring all the broken pieces of our lives to Jesus, He would give us a new life! But, we would have to bring God all the pieces!" I was stunned.

Many went forward for prayer. I didn't believe that saying unspoken words to an invisible person could make any difference in my life, but what did I have to lose? If it didn't work, I could always go back to being "normal!" So I gave God my will, but not my life!

My husband Roy who drove me to church, returned to pick me up from the meeting and we were both silent on the drive home. He was absorbed in driving, and I was deep in thought! Roy turned on the radio and Nelson Eddy was singing my favorite song, *The Indian Love Call*. While I had not responded to the Altar Call at the church, I was now listening to a call that I could neither hide nor run from. I was listening with my heart, not my brain and it was not Nelson Eddy, but Jesus singing to me!

> When I'm calling you, will you answer too?
> That means I offer my LOVE to you, to be your own.
> If you refuse Me, what will I do, loving you all alone?
> But, if when you hear My love call, ringing clear;
> And I hear your answering echo, so clear:
> Then I will know our Love will be true:
> You'll belong to Me;
> I'll belong to you!"

At that moment, I loved Jesus and gave Him my heart and my life!

E. STANLEY JONES:

"The Ordinary Becomes Extraordinary..."

The conversion of Mary seems to have been very quiet and unaccompanied by any cataclysm. It was like the opening of a flower to the sun. A young man inquired: "Do I have to have an experience as sudden and cataclysmic as Paul's in order to grow?" The answer from Mary's conversion experience is, No. She instinctively took to it (her conversion) as if it were her homeland, and at once she was at home.

Typically there is a separate and post-conversion experience of the filling of the Spirit. In Mary's case it seems all to have happened all at once. At any rate her subconscious mind seems to have been immediately "Christianized." Mary has the most Christian reactions to every situation that arises, and these reactions are instinctive and immediate. She puts it this way: "God seems to press the right button within me at the right time." For instance, as she sat at the table in a highly cultured family, a young man, who was attending a university, said in response to something Mary said: "I don't believe all that." The mother was mortified at her son's reaction, but Mary, without batting an eye, said: "But that is what is precious about you, Frank; you don't swallow everything you hear, and you shouldn't! You should keep an open mind and test things for yourself; then no one can fool you with false ideas." Frank smiled, and Mary had him; she got behind his defenses, effortlessly.

A skeptical doctor said when someone described Mary as ordinary looking: "Well, she has something I've never seen before, and it makes her beautiful." Even a little child can see it. One day she was sitting in a railway waiting room, and a little dirty-faced urchin came up and sat beside her and without a word put up his shoe to be tied. She tied it. And then he put up his other shoe to be tied. She tied it and then patted his leg. He got down, came around and patted her on the cheek, and then ran off. The spectators smiled, and some could scarcely keep back the tears. Love had become incarnate, and a child saw it.

MARY WEBSTER:

I went to bed after I got home from the Church wondering how this "New Life" would begin, and, if I would experience any change. I soon fell asleep only to be awakened by God! He told me to go downstairs and kneel beside my couch. I was not to turn on any light as God was going to turn one on inside of me, so bright, there would be no need for electricity. This would be my first miracle and I obeyed Him without question!

Kneeling by the couch, God asked me what was the worst sin I had ever committed? My tears initially kept me from answering, but then I began to confess to every sin that I had ever committed and every lie I had ever told, until I was broken and sobbing. "I'm not fit to live," I said. God answered: "Who ever told you that you were living? You were only existing! From now on I'll show you what real life is all about." After a little more sleep, I awoke completely rested. This was not at all like me, as usually, I would not get up early. My husband, Roy, a farmer, was up at 4:30 a.m. to feed the animals and milk the cows. Most farmer's wives would have a hot breakfast ready for their husbands when they came back from the barn. That was not what I did. Roy would get his own breakfast and mine, if I wasn't up yet. I thought I was lucky. However, that morning the Lord said to me: "Get up and get your husband's breakfast. You are not "lucky" –you are lazy. I'm going to save your marriage as well as your life."

Then a second miracle occurred. I got up, got dressed, and fixed Roy a hot breakfast. When he came in, the shock was almost too much for him! He didn't understand what was happening to me (and to him) but he loved it! Jesus had told me not to tell anyone that I had become a Christian. Roy began to watch me. My four year-old son, Claudie, spilled his glass of milk all over my nice clean tablecloth and I didn't explode as I typically did when someone made a mess. Roy knew

> **Jesus was not only saving me; He was saving Claudie from me! And that was a lot of saving!**

something had happened to me and so did Claudie. My son said, "What's got into you, Mommy? You used to yell like the old witch in a fairy when I spilled my milk."I patted him on the head and said, "Just the love of Jesus, honey."He then said, "Man, I love Jesus! He'll make a good woman out of you yet!"Jesus was not only saving me; He was saving Claudie from me! And that was a lot of saving!

Even my chickens knew something had happened to me. My usual habit, when gathering the eggs, was to reach in the nest, grab the hen by the neck and throw her off the nest. Then, I'd pick up the eggs. The hens would peck my hand in return. Roy asked me why I always attacked the chickens instead of just getting the eggs. He said he could always tell when I was in the hen house, for the chickens were squawking; feathers flying; and a cloud of dust was coming out of the hen house! The next morning when I went to the hen house, I knocked on the door and said, "Girls, I'm coming in, but I'm not the same old witch that's been wringing your necks. I am a Christian now. I have come to thank you for all of your hard work in laying the eggs." The hens stood up and seemed to say: "Help yourself. We like you when you come in this way."Not one hen tried to peck me. I got the eggs without any dust flying about! The hens even began laying double-yoked eggs! They were almost too large for the egg case. The only thing that changed was my attitude toward them. The chickens must have been so glad I had become a Christian.

A few days later, Roy was talking to the man who brought gasoline to our farm. They were discussing the miracles of Christ. The gas man said he didn't believe in miracles. Roy said: "Well, I don't know about you, but, Christ has gotten my wife to make my breakfast and that's miracle enough for me!" Two weeks later, Roy went to church with me! He went to the altar and surrendered his life to Christ. He told the Pastor that only God could change a woman as He had me. God had changed me 100% and Roy wanted that God to be his God!

E. STANLEY JONES:

Mary once told me the following:

> "Before my conversion I was trying to live 'in spite of,' but after reading your book, *The Way to Power and Poise,* the very Power you wrote about began to change the words 'in spite of' to 'because of,' and everything within me began to mellow. My attitude before I surrendered my life to Christ was that of defiance: 'I don't care "life" what you do to me... I'm determined to live in spite of anything you can do to stop me.' But after reading *The Way to Power and Poise* I was taken to what the aviators call 'the point of no return.' I didn't have enough fuel left in my tank to go back to where I started and couldn't just stay suspended in mid-air, so out of sheer necessity I had to go on to Christ. Christ brought me back alive, and now I can look life straight in the face and say, 'Dear precious life, I had you all wrong! I no longer tolerate you, I accept you just as you come.' Now life and I are no longer at swords' points with each other. We are friends, and the more I invest in life, the greater are the dividends that I receive."

Mary shares a great principle of human living: Don't be at swords' points with life, tense and anxious and defensive; accept what comes from life and make something out of it. A theological professor, known for his soundness of thought and emotional stability, and the last person on earth you would expect to be swept off his feet, came into the room and danced around the room with his hands up in the air after a talk with Mary and said: "For once I've seen a child of the Kingdom." She is just that, the most natural and the most naturalized child of the Kingdom I have seen in my travels around the world. Her growth in less than three years of living a Christian life has been so astonishing that one very able woman said of Mary, "She is growing alarmingly."

And yet you can see Mary's growth is no seven-day-wonder type of growth. It is all so natural, so sane, and so with-its-feet-on-the-ground. Mary offers this simple statement about the way she grows:

> When I was talking with Jesus tonight, He told me He was going to help me grow inwardly. He said that the most important thing to remember is always to keep my eyes on Him, and listen to Him when the going gets tough. He said He wanted me to learn to be patient when it is difficult to be patient, to be cheerful and happy when others are grouchy and sour. He wants me to learn to stop when He says, 'That's enough,' and to go when He says, 'The road is clear.' He wants me to see, in each distasteful thing that I'm called on to do, an opportunity to grow, and that it is for Him that I labor and not for the world. He said He would never call me to do something when I could not, but that with the "call" would come the necessary power to do it.

We come now to the part of Mary's life when her "new" life met the supreme test. Would her life hold together when everything crashed around her and everything did crash around her. This is a letter written two weeks after an auto accident in which her husband was killed and Mary, her two sons and her sister-in-law were badly injured. I have received many thousands of remarkable letters. This is my most unforgettable letter.

Dear Brother Stanley:

Claudie has a bad skull fracture and is not too good. His legs began to get stiff yesterday, and he can't turn over without experiencing a great deal of pain. The hospital staff is watching him closely. How grateful I am that God healed my wounds enough so that I have strength enough to come and stay with Claudie. My hand has a few fractures and also my ribs on the left side, but my leg wasn't broken, nor my jaw, as they first thought. I was cut with glass, but I'm still "on top of the heap." I'm still very sore and bruised all over, but otherwise just fine! I am trying hard, with grace from God, not to worry about Claudie's condition, but to just trust and keep my mind free, so I can help him all I can. He really needs a strong mother now, and I know God will help me be strong, for He has already done miracles for me.

Brother Stanley, ever since a year ago at the silent Communion service, I've understood what death really is and have tried to tell others just how beautiful an experience it will really be. It seemed to me at the Communion service that I had a glimpse of eternity, and it was so beautiful my heart nearly broke with joy and rapture.

Well, it is one thing to tell someone something, and another thing to go through the experience. I wondered if when my time came to "taste death," if it would hit me as an evil thing, or if it would still seem to be as beautiful as it was at that communion service. Now I can tell you with all sincerity that my original opinion has been strengthened! I can truthfully say that, at least for me, death doesn't have any "sting." This may seem strange to you, as it certainly has to so many others, especially the doctors and nurses.

Even when they told me Roy was killed, I didn't feel one bit like crying. I haven't shed a tear over it, nor do I feel like crying. God has been teaching me so much these last fifteen months, and He has so transformed my thinking that now I see this accident in its true light and not as an event that was designed to hurt me.

The truck that caused the accident was trying to pass another car, when the truck driver saw us coming toward him. He applied his brakes to slow down and tried to get back into his lane, but the wheels of his truck locked and threw him sideways in front of our car, and he hit us head on. The driver of the truck was utterly helpless, and it really was just an accident. Roy was killed instantly and so did not suffer. It is not tragic just because it happened to me. I know that when two cars going forty-five or fifty miles per hour hit head on, it is inevitable that someone gets hurt or killed. We just happened to be in the path of the truck. I certainly do not believe that it was God's will that we be hurt or that Roy be killed. However, because the laws of the universe are truly dependable laws, they work no matter who obeys them or breaks them. How grateful I am that this is so! And God was right with us after the accident. I saw Him in the faces of those who out of the compassion of their hearts helped us. I saw God in the eyes of the ambulance driver who could barely speak as he saw that his friend Roy was dead. I saw God in the doctors who instantly came to help us in the Emergency Room and worked for hours caring for our injuries. I saw the face of God in the friends, 400 of them at Roy's funeral; in Brother Loyal, who was at my bedside as soon as humanly possible; in the flowers and cards of sympathy from all over. Most of all I experienced God in that "still, small Voice" that said over and over again to me, "Be not afraid Mary, for I am with you always, even unto the end of the world," and then "I am the Resurrection and the Life, and whosoever lives and believes in me shall never die. Do you Mary believe me?" I replied: "Yes, my precious Lord, I do believe that You are the one true God of the living!" And from then on my soul has been completely free of all things but His own precious holy love.

Jesus has been with me every minute and I feel as if I have the wings of an eagle, and my heart is singing to the top of its voice our Ashram song: "I will not be afraid." It is a miracle that my dear, precious Jesus has performed in me, for while I thought it would be possible for me to accept death, little did I dream I

if you really do "keep your eyes upon Jesus," you can go through any storm life has and not have your spiritual equilibrium upset. But looking at Jesus and not at yourself makes the critical difference.

could rejoice and sing in the face of it! But you know it was not I, but He, who made this possible. All He has asked was that I just stay "open," and He has poured the blessings unto me! Life looks just as beautiful to me today as it did before the accident, because I have really discovered something wonderful; if you really do "keep your eyes upon Jesus," you can go through any storm life has and not have your spiritual equilibrium upset. But looking at Jesus and not at yourself makes the crucial difference.

43

I read in the Bible these words: "Mary has chosen that good part that shall not be taken from her."(Luke 10:42) I have chosen that "good part" of my husband that no one can ever take away from me. He is "one" with me now in the spirit of our Lord. It is as if he had just gone upstairs to rest, and I'll go too when I finish what I am doing, and we shall see each other again in the morning. So do not pity me. I find it impossible to pity myself.

Your prayers for me were certainly answered, for never have I felt the presence of God so strongly as in this past week. My faith in God is twice what it was (before the accident), and I feel relaxed even about Claudie. I know that God is even more interested in Claude's welfare than am I, and so everything will be fine.

All the doctors and nurses at the hospital were talking about what happened to me, for they had never seen anyone look death in the face and not bat an eye. When I told them what God had done for me and what I thought death was, they said they felt so much better, for they had always feared death. They were certain I was telling the truth because my reaction was so consistent with my words. They even thought that they would start going to church again. When God enters the picture, glory breaks all around!

The hardest part was telling Teddy about his daddy. It was like running a long, sharp dagger into his little heart, but he will get over it, for he took it like a soldier. I have yet to tell Claudie about his father's death, but I will when he is well again.

Your happy sister, Mary.

44

MARY WEBSTER:

I don't remember anything about the accident. However, while I was apparently unconscious, Jesus came into the car and said, "I am the resurrection, and the life: he who believes in me, shall have eternal life. He who believeth in me, though he were dead, yet shall he live: and whosoever liveth and believeth in me shall never die. Believest thou this?" (John 11:25) I answered, "I believe it in my head, but I don't know it in my experience. If you Lord, came out of your tomb, please bring me out of mine! Take me from just believing to really knowing! Show me, in my life and heart, that the resurrection is true and it is real!" God did!

The next day, I was surprised to see, in the doorway of my room, the pastor of the largest church in the city! (I had met him recently at a retreat where, the subject of death was discussed. I had asked him why, if we Christians say we believe in the resurrection, do we cry and carry on so when friends and family members die? The pastor asked me if I had ever lost anyone I loved. I had to admit I had not. He told me to wait until I had, and I would know what grief causes people to do.) I invited him into my hospital room, but asked him to leave his sorrowful looking face behind for I had Good News for him. He could no longer tell me I didn't know what I was talking about when it came to grief because now I had moved from believing in the resurrection, to knowing it (is real) from personal experience!

The pastor fell on his knees beside my bed and wept. He said he had dreaded coming to see me after my husband's death. He thought I had a "Pollyanna" approach to death. He expected me to be broken in spirit, not radiant, and certainly not witnessing to the Resurrection! He said he had never before offered anyone his pulpit on Easter Sunday. However, he asked me to take his pulpit on Easter Sunday because I knew the Resurrection was real and, he only "believed" in it. So I did!

Later, I heard two doctors discussing me! I pretended to be asleep so I could listen to their conversation. Neither knew anything about me, nor my emotional status. They needed to tell me that my husband had died but thought that if I were unstable and given this information that it might be a shock to my system and be dangerous to my health. But if they waited until I came out of my delirium and then told me, it would also be a shock and potentially dangerous as well. They came into my room accompanied by two nurses.I asked if they were going to tell me that my husband was dead. They said, "Yes."I said, "Well, my husband is a Christian, so he now has Eternal Life; and that means, he isn't really dead!" They looked at each other and said:"Let's go! She's really in shock!"I called after them and said:"No, I'm not in shock, I'm in Christ!"

The nurses later commented that they had never seen anyone look death in the face and never bat an eye. They thought they should go back to church to see what they had missed. I said however, that I wasn't looking at death. I was looking at Jesus. I wasn't holding on to Him; He was holding on to me! I had been given His strength!

During the accident, Claudie, my youngest son, was thrown from the back seat into the front seat and hit his head on a large metal ashtray on the dashboard, which caused a major skull fracture! The doctor told me Claudie's injuries were so severe and he had lost so much blood, that he had only a 50-50 chance of surviving the needed brain surgery. I prayed, "Jesus, I'm afraid for my son's life! I don't know how to pray about this. The mother part of me wants to beg You to save him but the Christian part of me, wants to trust that You will do what is best for him! This is too big for me to handle!"I did know, however, how to trust Jesus and so I went to Claudie's bed, put my hands under his little body, and said:"Jesus, I offer You my child whom I love with all my heart. I will not tell You what to do. Your plans are always perfect.

They looked at each other and said:"Let's go! She's really in shock!"I called after them and said:"No, I'm not in shock, I'm in Christ!"

Please receive my son as my love offering to You, with no strings attached. If he survives the operation but is damaged in some on-going way, show me how to handle it. If he doesn't survive the operation, I will accept that. I release him completely into Your protective, loving care. Amen."

A great peace came over me! The morning of the surgery I said to Claudie, "Honey, today you are going to have a great adventure! The doctor is going to give you something to put you to sleep, and, you will dream. You may even dream in color. Be sure to remember your dream, so that you can tell me about it."

The nurse came in with the sedative but was trying to hide the needle from Claudie. He saw it and said to her,

47

"What are you going to do with that needle you are hiding?"She said: "I am going to stick it in your arm!"He rolled up his sleeve, and said: "Well nurse, just do it!" He held out his arm and took the sedative injection.I wheeled him to the operating room, kissed him and said: "Remember your dream!" He waved and said: "I will!" Five hours later, he was brought back to his room. He was so pale that I thought that he had died! However, an hour later, he was sitting up asking for soda and ice cream. The doctor said that Claudie was an excellent patient! The doctor added, "In all operations, there are two doctors, one to operate and one to assist in case of emergency. Today, there were three! I know who that third one was, and HE made all the difference!"

There were some legal complications after the car accident, which I want to share. The driver of the pickup truck was the only person in this accident, (which had caused one death and five persons to be hospitalized) who was not injured. Following the accident, he was arrested and put in jail. However, since I would not press charges, he was released. A lawyer said I should go to court to secure a settlement. I told him that as a Christian, I would not sue another person. The lawyer tried to convince me that I now had children to support and because the driver was "responsible" it was only right and fair to sue him. I responded, that I would have to pray about it and see what God wanted me to do. When I prayed, the Lord asked me if I had ever broken any motor vehicle laws. I said that I had but was not caught. The Lord reminded me that then I was not in a very good position to sue this man but I was in a wonderful position to forgive him!

When I went to court the next day, I told the lawyer

48

that I wanted to settle out of court and that I would accept the insurance company offer of $18,000. The lawyer tried to push me to ask for more. I told him, "I had talked to God about it and I was not to sue the driver of the truck that hit our car, but to forgive him. It was a case of bad judgment on the driver's part. He didn't mean to do it! So I can't sue him." The lawyer said: "You have rocks in your head!" I replied, "That may be so, but I have Jesus in my heart!" The driver was in the courtroom so I went over to him and said: "I have some really good news for you! God doesn't hold this car accident against you, and neither do I! Jesus is the very best friend you ever had! He is your SAVIOR and he is saving you from me, and that is a lot of saving!"

The driver was astonished, and said: "You mean you aren't going to sue me? You don't want me to go to jail? You don't want to make me pay for what I have done?" I told him that Jesus "paid" for "everything" and asked me to forgive him! The driver burst into tears and said: "I just knew you would sue me and would want to get even with me! But you didn't, because you love Jesus! I'll love Him forever for that. I will give Him my heart and life!"

My sister-in-law, Aunt May, was hospitalized after the accident for eight months. When she was finally released, the doctor suggested she go to a nursing home where she could continue to receive care. I told him that instead of going to a nursing home, she could come home with me. If she required nursing care, we would hire a nurse. If tender, loving care was all that was needed, the boys and I could supply that. She wanted to stay with us, and we became the same happy family we were before the accident. We shared everything. I was so happy to have her home again, that I gladly provided whatever care she needed. I loved her and wanted to make her comfortable and happy.

E. STANLEY JONES:

The Menial Becomes a Sacramental

While Mary did serve as a loving caretaker for Aunt May, there were some things involved in taking care of her "sister" (she never calls her "sister-in-law") that Mary didn't like. Mary told me:

> The Lord said to me, 'Mary, I know you don't like to do certain things involved in nursing, but I want to do them for her and I can't. I haven't anyone else to provide care for Aunt May, except you. Will you do these things for My sake?' That transformed everything involving Aunt May's care into a sacrament. It's a joy now to do it for His sake.

I want my sister to be as happy and content as I am, and I pray God will show me all the little ways of making her serene and happy for the rest of her days. He will, and he has, and I've learned that to really love Jesus you must love, cherish and serve what He loves, cherishes and serves. And once His love invades your heart, it all becomes automatic, for in each small task you see an opportunity of saying, 'I love You, Jesus', and then the care is no longer a task but a privilege. Blessed, blessed Jesus!

Then Mary adds this observation:

> "There is no success in life, only fulfillment. Nothing could

be more glorious and more exciting in all the world than just what I am doing right now, right here; and that is just being useful and loving to one human being out of love for Him and gratitude for the privilege or serving another. . . . This is my mission field. I love it."

MARY WEBSTER:

One day as I was leaving the living room, I had the "misfortune" of overhearing guests saying, "Isn't Mary a wonderful little Christian! She is so good to Aunt May. "I heard those compliments and I, egocentrically, began to believe them. It was no longer a privilege to care for Aunt May but a duty. I began to hate giving her baths. I hated emptying her bedpan. I did it lovingly as long as there was an audience but when there was no one to watch me, I just reacted! I didn't even realize what was happening to me.

One night, as I left May's room to empty the bedpan, I burst into tears, fell on my knees and cried, "Jesus, I can't do this anymore. Isn't there something more "religious" that I could do for You? I am not a nurse, so, please, get me a replacement." Jesus said:"I

There is no success in life, only fulfillment. Nothing could be more glorious and more exciting in all the world than just what I am doing right now, right here; and that is just being useful and loving to one other human being out of love for Him and gratitude for the privilege or serving another.

know all about this situation. I know you have begun to hate now doing what you once did out of love. But, I never get tired of helping people who are immobile or need help. I want to help Aunt May and you are the only person I have to do it. Couldn't you do it for Me?" I was so ashamed of myself and I remembered Jesus' words: "In as much as you do it unto one of the least of these, you do it even so unto Me." It was then that I realized that every act of kindness or unkindness I did to someone else, I first did it to Jesus. That realization made all the difference.

I went back into Aunt May's bedroom a different person because I had been with Jesus. It wasn't my duty rather it was my privilege to offer these small acts of caring for Aunt May. I asked her, "Aunt May, would you like for me to give you a backrub?" She said: "Honey, you are so good to me and, you do so much for me, I wouldn't want to add to your many burdens but, if you have the time and the energy, I would love to have my back rubbed!" As I began to rub her back she said: "Mary you have the touch of an angel. When the nurse at the hospital rubbed my back, she did it as a job, but you do it out of love for me!" I thought, if she only knew who was rubbing her back, she would get up and walk! As I looked at her back, I knew it was really Jesus' back. I looked at my hands, they were not my hands, they were the hands of Jesus! When I looked at her, I didn't see her, I saw Jesus! The whole room was filled with His love and His spirit! I suddenly remembered the words carved across our Communion table: "Do this in remembrance of Me." I had asked Jesus to carve those words across my heart!

E. STANLEY JONES:

Here is another revelation of Mary's spirit:

> I have been studying the subject of "humility." God finds me a very difficult student, for I just don't understand the word in all its fullness. God told me to find something each day to do that is beneath me; but there's where I'm in checkmate, as they say in chess. I just can't seem to find anything that is beneath me. What could it be?

Her simplicity of motive and humility come out in this sentence: "I found I didn't want to use Jesus to ask for special favors. I just want to love Him for nothing." "To love Him for nothing" is the pure, flame of a purified devotion and love.

MARY WEBSTER:

When I was eleven months old, my mother was killed in an accident on an excursion boat. She didn't want to go on the boat, but my father insisted. The boat sank and dozens of people perished, including my mother. My mother's relatives implied that she would still be alive, if it were not for my father! So there was a fear inside of me about him and for years I withheld myself from a relationship with him.

One day while I was on my way to Boston to help Brother Stanley, I learned that my father was dying, and that I must come home immediately! I was not very happy about it as I was looking forward to going to Boston. I had been a Christian for seven years but it never crossed my mind to tell my father, (the one person I judged the most harshly) about Jesus who could forgive him and save him! I thought, as I drove to my father's home, what I would say to him. I'd tell him God would forgive all his sins and that God loved him! It was a great speech! However, when I arrived, I was really upset! My father wasn't dying! He wasn't even sick! I had really wanted to go to Boston and so felt duped. It wouldn't be so easy to give my "great speech" to my father.

Soon after I arrived, Dad had to walk to town for something so, I walked along beside him intending to tell him about Jesus. But, I couldn't say one word of significance! We talked about the weather, baseball games, and a lot of trivia but not a word about Jesus! Later, my father went to sit in the garden and I sat down beside him, again wanting so very much to tell him about God, but no words would come out of me! Not a word was spoken between us that evening and I knew I had to leave in the morning and that I had not done what I came to do. I got on my knees and said: "Jesus, why can't I talk to my father when I can talk to total strangers about You?" He said: "Because of your attitude!"

I was shocked and asked, "What attitude?" Jesus said: "Why did I ask you to come home? Not to have you tell your father that I will forgive him. I can tell him that myself! I brought you here for one reason, for you to tell your father that you love him and forgive him! And you need to ask him to forgive you!" I was shocked! "Forgive me? For what! I've never done anything to him!" Jesus said: "That is why you are to ask him to forgive you. You have never even heard his side of the story. You judged him from what others told you. You withheld your love from him. You didn't want to come home! You were upset because his "dying" interfered with your plans. You haven't been a very good daughter. Tell him how sorry you are and ask him to forgive you!"

I didn't sleep a wink that night for I dreaded the morning to come. After breakfast, my dad went out to sit under the apple tree. I went outside as well and knelt down in front of my father. I was so ashamed that I didn't dare look at him. I buried my head in his lap as tears streamed down my face. I began "Daddy, I didn't want to come here. I remembered that the last time I was with you, you were not a Christian. I became a Christian seven years ago but, not once did it occur to me to come home and tell you about Jesus. I only came this time to tell you God loves you and will forgive you of all your sins. On our walk to town, I tried to say something but I could not. When I went to bed, Jesus told me to ask you to forgive me and give me another chance. I have been so unloving and judgmental."

> "Jesus, why can't I talk to my father when I can talk to total strangers about You?" He said: "Because of your attitude!"

My father seldom showed any emotion but now he burst into tears and held me ever so close to him. He said: "Oh, you poor little girl. The last time I saw you, I knew you were not a Christian as you were bitter and full of resentments. Seven years ago, I became a Christian as well, and, I have prayed for God to "save" you. I knew that unless you thought I was dying, you would not come home. I wanted to talk to you about God. On our walk to town, I tried to bring it up but no words came out of my mouth either. I didn't sleep last night, asking God why I couldn't talk to my own child about Him? You were trying to convert me and I was trying to convert you! If we had looked at each other through Jesus, instead of judgment, we would have seen Jesus in each other!

"There, at the foot of the old apple tree, I found my father! But, more than that, I found my Heavenly Father! I had never referred to God as "Father." That word was too painful! I didn't want my Heavenly Father to be like my father was! Now, I loved the word."

E. STANLEY JONES:

Mary has preached from some major pulpits. One of them was in a large African American church. She writes:

> The fact that it was an African-American church was one of the main reasons for my wanting so much to go. I was so happy they would let me come and not hold my race against me. I worked on my sermon for the whole two hour train ride, for it was to be a great talk. As I stood up, I paused a moment, sizing up my audience, and do you know what I saw? I saw Jesus take my speech and tear it into tiny bits and throw them away, and then He said: "Mary, you were called to witness, not to give a speech. Look into My face and tell them what you see."

And the message just spoke itself, without any notes, or any effort on my part. When I finished, one of the sisters came up and took me in her arms and kissed me on the cheek. It was so tender and soul trembling, that I thought I would never want to wash that cheek again, lest I destroy the beauty of such a blessing. At that moment there wasn't any question of race; it was just one child of

God loving another and meaning it! And it came to me that being one in Him is the perfect solution of the so-called race problem!

MARY WEBSTER:

Five months after I surrendered my life to Jesus, I attended my first Christian Ashram in Kerrville, Texas. While there I met a black lady named Arrah. Never having been in the south before, I wasn't aware of the customs. I didn't know anything about segregation. I had never met a black person before I met this wonderful lady.

Before leaving the Ashram to go home, we all joined hands, and said to each other, "Unreservedly given to God; unbreakably given to each other!" I really meant these words as I said them to my new friend, Arrah. After the Ashram several of us went to the bus station to begin our journeys' home. To my great delight, Arrah was there as well. She said she was going to my destination, "Oh great!" I said, "You and I can sit together and talk about the Ashram." She said:"I'm sorry, we can't do that, we are in Texas!" I said: "I know we are in Texas, but I don't understand if we are going to the same place, on the same bus, breathing the same air, and are new best friends, what difference does it make where we sit?" She told me there was a white line on the floor in the back of the bus and black people had to sit behind it! Then I said: "Then I'll come and sit with you!" She said:"That isn't a good idea. Do you see those two ladies over there? They were at the Ashram when we joined hands and made our pledge. Not once, have they looked in my direction. As long as they don't look at me, they don't have to deal with the "race" problem. We all know the "game" and how to play it."

As we started to board the bus I began to hear Satan's voice, "Sit in the white section like you are supposed to do. Remember the thirteenth commandment, mind your own business!" Then St. Peter countered and said: "Are you going to make the same mistake I did? Haven't you learned anything from my example? I told Jesus in the Upper Room that everyone would desert Him, except me! However, I was the only one who did! Remember my shame and regret? An hour ago you said you were unbreakably given to Arrah. Are you now going to pretend you don't know her?"I handed the driver my ticket and made my way to the back of the bus, where Arrah was sitting on the aisle. I told her to move over, that I was going to sit there. She told me to sit on the inside as the driver might not see me!

The driver got on the bus and looked right at me! Living on a farm, I've learned that when you bring in the cows from the pasture, the thing to do is to look them straight in the eye and let them know who is boss. So I determined to look the driver in the face and said to myself, (I would have said it out loud if needed...) "I'm obeying a law higher than the law of this state, the law of the Kingdom of God." But he just looked at me for a long time, then shrugged his shoulders and sat down to drive! My seatmate said:"Thank the Lord, Honey, for illustrating the real thing that you get at the Ashram."

E. STANLEY JONES:

People respond to "Mary's" simplicity and her disarming, unaffected loving ways. She writes:

For quite some time now I've noticed that everybody I meet calls me by my first name! Recently a very austere man, a superintendent of schools, asked me to come to his office. He kept me for two hours discussing religion. And he called me 'Mary' the whole time! He is an intellectual and kept asking over and over again, 'How?' I told him how I met Christ and about what has happened to me since then. He listened and said he would like to feel inside the way my face looked on the outside. He wants joy, of course, but only Christ within can produce that joy! It all seems so simple, but often it is very difficult to get the real message across to others. They typically approach the step of 'surrender' and then try going down a side alley instead of going that one step forward to the Way."

When God has a message to give to the world, He uses the first available instrument He finds regardless of its "defects" or capacity.

Mary's words are simple, but very, very effective. Her eager spirit of simple obedience is revealed in this comment, "I don't want a thing explained now, so much as I want it revealed." The revelation is enough for Mary.

MARY WEBSTER:

Nothing anyone says to me can insult me or hurt my feelings any more, for there is nothing anyone can say to me that I haven't already said to myself; and no one can flatter me anymore, because no matter what anyone says, there is always the picture in my mind of what I was before

59

Christ, while all they see is what has happened to me after Christ. When God has a message to give to the world, He uses the first available instrument He finds regardless of its "defects" or capacity. While God might have wanted someone strong he found me instead "a bruised and broken reed." That is the reality and God will use me until something better comes along. He may want a light and I'm just a dimly burning wick. But still He'll use me, limited as I might be.

E. STANLEY JONES:

A friend writes about Mary: "She is rare indeed. All her discernments are immaculate." They are straight from God. Mary writes:

> But in the name of Jesus, Brother Stanley, please expect big things of me and help me to surpass your expectations! I'm not asking for flattery; I'm begging you to take me out of the safety zone, where nothing happens, and take me to that point of no return where everything can happen. There are big things to be done in this world that won't wait forever, so that's why I ask you to dream up the greatest possible thing you can think of that a woman can do and share your dream with me, and then hand me the pick and shovel and tell me to go to work.

During the period of gathering material for this book (*Growing Spiritually*) I wrote to her and asked her to send me any material she came across which I could use. Her reply was characteristic: "Brother Stanley, if you come across any new ideas, send them to me, and I'll put them in practice to see whether they will work. I'll be your guinea pig for ideas." And she would do just that! She wrote: "When you say to audiences that they are 'to go out and give out love and only love, and if it doesn't work, increase the dose,' they usually laugh, but I went out and did just that, and it worked."

MARY WEBSTER:

I broke my right arm in an accident and needed therapy twice a week to help increase my arm's mobility. Since I traveled most of the time, it was impossible to have treatment from a different therapist each time, so I had to either give up my work or give up therapy. However, the therapist said my arm would soon become stiff and unusable without continued therapy. What did I want to do — stay home and be treated or, leave and have a stiff right arm the rest of my life? I kept traveling.

Months later, I was holding a meeting in a small church. It was a morning meeting with the women of the church. They were holding a Healing Service and formed a large circle of chairs, with one chair in the middle of the circle. If you needed prayer for healing you could sit on that chair. Different group members would come and lay hands on you as the whole group prayed for your healing. Before we went to the meeting, I had told some of the women about my arm being so stiff and that I couldn't get my thumb to my mouth. However, I decided not to sit in the "healing" chair. I was determined that I could get along very well with the arm as it was. With our heads bowed, we prayed for the lady in the chair who had cancer. As I was praying for her, God said to me, "Stretch out your right arm." I told Him it just wouldn't go out. Again He said: "Stretch out your right arm." He repeated the

61

words, "stretch out your right arm." I shut my eyes and stretched my arm out as far as I could, and then a strange thing happened. I felt someone pulling my arm out full length and it sounded like someone was breaking kindling. The pain was terrible and tears were running down my face. Nobody was touching me but, one lady said, as the arm was straightening out, "Oh, Lord, don't make it longer than the other one." At this, everyone stopped to see what was going on. My arm became scarlet and I could stretch it out just as far as the other one. Everyone was amazed at what happened to me but no one could explain it! You can't explain miracles; you can only thank God for doing His work, in His mysterious ways, and be grateful in your heart!

E. STANLEY JONES:

This passion for growth and improvement does not leave her concentrated on herself. This sentence reveals her spirit: "I want to put everything I have into life and take out only what I need."

We come now to look at Mary's amazing joy. She is the purest sparkling fountain I've ever seen. Hers is not a surface joy; it is a joy that has met the worst and has turned it into something else, something higher. She writes:

"Brother Stanley, He is so marvelous to me that I can scarcely tell it to anyone. He amazes me with all that He gives me and does to me and with me. It is like a fairy story come true. I'm like a pumpkin that He has touched with His magic wand and turned into a lovely carriage. You've probably heard the story of the child who had a fan (the hand type), and she showed it to a famous painter, who said:"Let me have your fan, and I'll paint a beautiful picture on it." She grabbed it back and said:"Give me the fan. It's mine, and I'll not let you spoil it." How often do we tell God, "This is my life. You might spoil it if you paint something on it." But oh, the unspeakable joy and glory that come when we learn to say, "Here am I, Lord, use me!"

And it is a joy that shows itself in loving service. Her sister-in-law was overheard telling some visiting relatives: "Mary is getting sweeter and sweeter every day. Whenever she does anything for me, she acts as though I'm doing her a favor to let her do it."

A grocer said to her, "Mary, you look happier than anyone else I ever saw. Have you some deep, dark secret you're hiding?" And she replied, "I sure have," and then whispered, "I love the Lord! And if you try it, it will put a bloom on your cheek like a sixteen-year-old." A druggist kept watching her out of the corner of his eye. She had something different. Then he blurted out, "Why are you so darn happy?" And she told him her secret. She writes: Our souls must be elastic, or mine would burst with sheer joy. ... I've learned what true happiness is -true and lasting happiness is just another name for God!

Again she writes: "You're right about my living on my knees! But you can't kiss His blessed feet and stand! I'm so glad of that."

A very earth-bound of minister said to her, "Mary, you scare me. Why, the world will crucify you if you go on thinking the way you do! You know, you have the warmth of a Methodist; the stubbornness of a Baptist; the straightlacedness of a Presbyterian; the enthusiasm of a Jehovah's Witness; and the common sense of a Congregationalist." And she replied, "Thank you for that lovely compliment, for you have just described me as a walking example of federal union (of the Church) which I believe in one hundred per cent." She is never without an answer. God always touches the

63

right button in her.

An infinite sanity runs through all she does. She writes: "As the physical grows in intensity, the mental grows in wisdom, and the spiritual grows in understanding of how to use it for growth in grace."

Mary makes everything she experiences contribute. This is characteristic: "Pain produces two opposites. One man rots in prison, while Paul writes holy scripture in prison. So it is not what happens, but how we interpret what happens to us. We do have the power of choosing not what happens to us, but how we let it affect us!"

Mary feels that she is not the source of things but only the channel and that God speaks to her directly. And He does! She says: "A watch doesn't create time, it simply registers it. A violin doesn't create music, it simply registers the music in the violinist. So we don't create, we transmit." She is the clearest channel of transmission I've ever seen. She says: "God's whole education of me is to improve my insights through my eyesight." This is a profound comment. Some of her insights break out into clear prose and some into poetry:

> As man's created spirit,
> Up the ladder, God-ward mounts,
> He finds it isn't altitude,
> But attitude that counts.

Then this:

> If you've never felt the sorrow
> Of another person's grief;
> If you've never felt an inner urge
> To want to bring relief
> To someone who's in trouble

64

By a kindly word or smile;
If you've never loved your neighbor
As yourself, with all your might;
If you've never shed a tear drop
At a pure and holy sight;
If you've never met your Savior-
You have nothing then to dread;
You need have no fear of dying,
Brother, you're already dead.

MARY WEBSTER:

The pastor of the church where I was to hold a meeting picked me up in his car to drive me to the church. On the way, he pulled over to the curb and parked in front of a house. He said he had to make a house call on a woman (Rebecca) who had been on a five-day drinking binge and was now very ill. The pastor asked me to wait in the car, as he would not be very long. I asked him if I might go with him. He said he didn't know what we would find but that I could come in with him. We went in the house and then into Rebecca's room. It was a mess and she was a mess. She looked so very pathetic. I got right up in the bed with her and put my arms around her and told her how sorry I was that she was so ill! We explained that we had to go to a meeting but we would come back to see her right afterward. The pastor then prayed for her and we left.

We returned later and again, I got up in the bed with her. She was afraid I would get my dress dirty. I assured her it was washable. I told her that if she truly wanted to stop drinking, God could deliver her from it. I told her I knew that she couldn't do it alone but God could do it for her without any effort! However, she had to really want to be delivered, as God would not do anything against her will! She cried and said: "Oh, I do want to be delivered, but I can't stop!" I responded, "I know honey, you can't but God can and will deliver you!"I took a small mirror from my purse that had a picture of Jesus on one side. I put it (Jesus side up) at the top of her bed. I told her that Jesus would be watching over her all night, and He was putting an angel at each corner of her bed so that no evil thing could touch her! There was a bottle half full of liquor on a table near the bed. I was about to take it away but Jesus said:"Leave it there!" We left Rebecca's house.

The next morning I was at the church for a breakfast meeting. When my food was served and I started to eat, the strangest thing happened! The coffee, toast, butter, everything... tasted and smelled like Rebecca's breath I thought the cook must have put alcohol into all the food! I told the pastor we needed to leave the church and go to see Rebecca immediately.

We went back to Rebecca's home and into her bedroom where we saw that the half empty bottle was still in the same place and still half empty! Rebecca was sitting up in bed and smiling. I asked her what happened! She said that all night long she wanted a drink in the worst way but she couldn't get to the bottle. Something kept her from it. Jesus was talking to her all night and by morning she didn't even want anything to drink! The liquor was there but she was free of it! She couldn't believe it! But neither could she doubt it!

Just then, as we were thanking God for His wonderful deliverance of Rebecca, her husband and son came in the room. They knelt on each side of the bed and asked her forgiveness for their lack of love and concern. Her husband told her he was going to pray and ask God to deliver him as well. Her son kissed her and said:"Mom, please forgive me for forgetting how good you have always been to me for 18 years. I love you and you and I are going to ride our bikes together, go on picnics, and have fun like we used to do!"The "work" was done and so we left. I kept in touch with the Pastor and learned that Rebecca's family was the strongest Christian family in his church! They were each living for Christ and were a great inspiration to everyone! This just goes to prove that Jesus is Lord!

... if she truly wanted to stop drinking, God could deliver her from it. I told her I knew that she couldn't do it alone but God could do it for her without any effort!

E. STANLEY JONES:

We continue to study Mary's amazing joy. She wrote:

"I have trouble with one passage of Scripture: 'Blessed are they that mourn.' I don't really know how to mourn." And she meant it. She seems to pluck out of every happening a joy. And it is not the joy of untouched aloofness, she's in life to the depths and takes what comes. She comments: "It's friction that makes the auto tire go places. Without it the tire just spins around going nowhere." She welcomes "each rebuff that turns earth's smoothness rough."

One day Mary was nailing up some shelves, and the hammer struck not the nail but her finger and thumb and left them both badly bruised. Her boys were playing in another room, and she overheard one saying to the other, "Come on, Mom's hurt herself real bad, for she is no longer hammering, but she's singing real loud, 'Glory, Hallelujah.'" She rescues something "beautiful" out of everything. The alchemy of her radiant spirit turns the base metal of very ordinary happenings into the glory of the Kingdom.

Mary once said:

How I love Him! Brother Stanley. Several times when I was out in public, I'd be praying to Him, and He'd tell me something especially precious, and before I knew it, I had said out loud, "Oh, Lord, how I love you!" People would look at me as if I were stark raving mad! They thought I had been listening to what they had been saying, and of course, my reply didn't fit into what they had said! But Jesus just smiles. He knows I'm crazy - crazy about Him!

MARY WEBSTER:

In one of our large cities, I was the guest of a pastor and his wife for lunch at a very expensive restaurant and we were talking about Jesus. While we were waiting to be served, a waiter came over to me and handed me a business card.It was from a company executive. On the other side he had written: "Miss, about Jesus, would you come over here and tell me about Him?"I said to the pastor and his wife, "Come on, we have work to do!"We went over to his table and the business executive was initially very embarrassed! He told me that he had made a mistake calling me to come over. I said:"Sir, you have probably made all kinds of mistakes in your life but calling for Jesus, is not one of them! We are not going to go away, sir. We want to help you!"The executive then said:"The reason I called you over here was that I heard you talking about Jesus and how He helped you and others and I need help with my son. He is in big trouble and the only time he ever talks to me is when he is in trouble and wants me to get him out of it!" I said, "Sir, I suppose that is exactly your position with your Heavenly Father. You just want to use Him as your son uses you! If you were on good speaking terms with your Heavenly Father, you could ask anything and you would not be denied."He said:"Oh, I have gone too far from God to expect Him to help me!" I responded, "You are only one step away; just turn around ask Him to forgive you. God has never left you, even if you have left Him!" I told him that he should bow his head and ask Him right now!

We took his hands and we all bowed our heads and he asked Jesus to forgive him and restore a right relationship with him. When he finished, his face was glowing! Then the pastor told him he would send someone to help the son do the same thing. The pastor also told him he wanted to meet with him every morning for prayer and Bible study and that is what they did! In that very expensive restaurant, we ended up doing something far more important than dining!

E. STANLEY JONES:

How? That is the thing that people want to know. They are more or less convinced that it (Christianity) is true, but how do you get it? Mary Webster knew how to answer the "how" question. One evening Mary was sitting in the dining car of a train. It was late and she could not find a place to sit in the coach, so she went to the dining car. She sat down next to a man who offered her a cigarette. She said, "No thank you, I don't need it."

He offered her a drink. Again she said, "No thank you, I don't need it." He responded, "What do you mean, you don't need it?"

"Well," she said, "I don't need it, I have something better." He asked her, "Where have you been?" She responded, "Chicago." "What were you doing there?" "Speaking." "On what?" "On Religion." And he and his seatmates covered their glasses with their newspapers. She said, "You need not do that. It (alcohol) has nothing to do with what I am talking about." "All right" they said, "go ahead and talk to us about what you have." And she began and everyone in dining car was gathered around her listening, including the waiter and no one ordered a drink. One man said to her, "Where did you get this?" She replied, "At the foot of the cross." "How did you get to the foot of the cross?" "At the end of my rope." For two and one half hours, the whole dining car listened to this young woman describe the "how" of Christianity. That is what people really want to know.

MARY WEBSTER:

During one of the missions I attended, I was given an assignment to attend a breakfast where some very wealthy and very intelligent pople were dining. Since I was neither, I dreaded going to the breakfast, as I always felt inferior to such people. However, they were perfectly charming to me and I soon forgot my dread and began to enjoy myself. One man asked me, "What would you say to a man who has everything; a wonderful wife and chil-

70

dren, Christian parents, a wonderful reputation in his community, teaches Sunday School, is highly respected at his work but, has a second-hand experience of God?" I was completely caught off guard and I didn't know what to answer. He did have everything; he was charming and well educated, and so I just assumed that he had to be a Christian. What a mistake! I had assumed that since he was a Christian he didn't need a first hand experience of Christ.

I later visited with him and said, "You are the man with the second-hand experience of God, aren't you?" It caught him off guard. He said: "Yes, how did you know?" I said: "God told me. That is why I had to come to talk with you." I continued, "You know the story of the rich young ruler who asked Jesus what he must do to inherit eternal life. Jesus told him five things: go and take what you have and give it to the poor and come and follow Me. He told him to go, give, take -in order to come and follow Him. Your money is not the same problem as it was for the rich young ruler, for his was selfishness; while you

Every life holds a cross and a throne. Only the soul can decide, whether the throne is for self or Christ, and who will be crucified!

are a generous person. However, you are offering God your money instead of yourself. God has all the money in the world, but He doesn't have you. As soon as you surrender yourself to Jesus and accept Him as your Savior and Lord, you will pass from knowing about Jesus to knowing Him personally!

Think what it would mean to the young people in your city if you witnessed to the fact that you no longer have Jesus as resident in your life; now you have made Him "PRESIDENT! "Let's just kneel here beside your sofa and pray."We prayed together and I said, "Every life holds a cross and a throne. Only the soul can decide, whether the throne is for self or Christ, and who will be crucified!" I continued, "You have now put Jesus on the throne and have taken the cross for yourself and that is very pleasing to Jesus. You are no longer a second-hander! Now, you are a first-hander! I realize that it is perhaps not easy for you to receive by faith, but we all come to Jesus as beggars. All your life you have been able to give to others but now you have to the opportunity to receive from God."

Mary then told him, "When I first became a Christian, I didn't know how to pray or read the scriptures to keep me in His Presence! So God used the only area of my life open enough to receive from Him, which was popular music. Just this morning I heard a jukebox playing, "I'll get by as long as I have You."I said: "I surely will, Jesus!" Coming home in a fog one night and I sang, "Guess I'll always be lost in a fog without You Jesus!" "You know if you insert Jesus' name in everything you see or hear, it contributes sacred meaning to everything secular and keeps you in His Presence!"

I suggested that he play that simple game until all he would see or hear became sacred to him. Later, I received this letter from him, in which he said that his little boy was playing some records and the words of one were "My heart cried for you." He said he knew it was meant for him when he sang it to Jesus and it became a sacred hymn to him. And to think that all this blessing came because of

72

a breakfast that I did not want to attend because of my sense of inferiority! He later wrote me, "You are the gal that really gave me the "business." Why you gave me so much of your time, I don't know. However, I am glad and I am grateful. I have really stuck my neck out and have reached the "point of no return" so I'm going on with Jesus! My theme song has become "Blessed assurance, Jesus is mine."

E. STANLEY JONES:

We have had the privilege of looking deeply into the soul of the most radiant Christian I know. Mary met the catastrophe of the death of her husband the way she meets everything, big and small, with a radiance of spirit that transforms everything. One would have thought that she would have had a "sag" (following the car accident). It did not happen. While she was waiting for her son's surgery to finish, Mary saw a young woman weeping outside the door, and she asked her what was the matter and the woman told her that her husband was dying in the adjacent hospital room. Mary tried to comfort her, and the woman said bitterly, "Yes, but you've not lost your husband, so you can say that." And Mary told her very quietly that she had lost her husband a week before. Then the girl listened. She took the girl to the coffee shop, talked to her, and sent her back with her burden lightened and her tears dry. She did this on her way up to the operating room where her own son was hovering between life and death. Now after a year and a half she is more radiant than ever. She recently penned these verses.

I am not sad!
I know the joy of a heart's full surrender,
I am living in splendor: I am not sad.

73

I'm not alone!
I have God's love and His spirit to guide me.
He is walking beside me: I'm not alone.

This pure radiance and joy of Mary is not mere moonshine. It works itself out in concrete situations as Christian living. In the settlement for the accident the lawyer said that if the senior member of the firm were associated with the junior member as a codefendant, then instead of $18,000 she could get $25,000. "But," said Mary, "the driver might be legally responsible, but he was not morally responsible for the accident. So I can't do it." At the close the lawyer took her up to the judge, who said: "My dear woman, I'm glad to shake the hand of a real Christian."

MARY WEBSTER:

Along the road to Glory, I was surprised to find that what I wanted to happen (the will of God) was just my own will disguised!

In one of the Ashrams I attended, a wealthy lady from Texas gave Dr. Jones three thousand dollars to pay my way to go with him and our Bible teacher to India. I was certain that it was God's will for me to go or the money to pay for the trip would not have been provided! The trouble with my logic was that I had not asked God if He wanted me to go to India! I was afraid of what His answer would be! Finally, I got up the courage to ask God if He wanted me to go! God answered: "Why do you want to go?" No use trying to fool God, so I told Him the truth! I said, "I suppose so I can say I have been there!" God said: "Do you think it is worth three thousand dollars just for an ego trip for you?" Well, no, if He put it that way. Then I asked Him, "If I wasn't supposed to go, why was the money given and everyone else said that they wanted me to go?"

God explained that He works with lots of people and when he wants a certain thing to happen, he has to get a range of people ready for their part and may use some as catalytic agents. God told me: I want to use you as a catalytic agent now because you are willing to do my will without question. I used you to get the money to send Sten Nilsson, not you, as the donor doesn't know Sten and would not have offered the funds for his trip to India. He will be more help on the trip to India than you would be. He is going for the right reason and you just wanted to brag that you had been there. Do you remember the night you graduated from High School? You only had one living parent, your father, and he didn't go to see you get your diploma. You were so hurt and you said to Me, "I could never treat my child that way!" Now your young son, Claude is graduating from High School soon. You are the only living parent he has. Do you want to be half way around the world on an ego trip on the only day he will ever graduate from High school? I thought you said you would never do that to your child!"

> God explained that He works with lots of people and when he wants a certain thing to happen, he has to get a range of people ready for their part and may use some as catalytic agents.

I felt just awful and I told God I would tell Dr. Jones that I was not supposed to go, and that he was to ask Sten. He quickly agreed. The whole matter would have been a little easier to swallow if Brother Stanley had not agreed so quickly!

When I told my family that I was turning down the offer to go to India, they wondered why! I told my son that when I first considered it, I had forgotten that this was the year he would be graduating from High School and I wouldn't miss attending that for anything in this world! Claude came over and said tenderly, "Mom, you mean you love me that much to give up a trip around the world just to see me get that diploma!" I hugged him and told him I loved him a lot more than that! Later, I went around the world three times. When I took those trips, I was ready to go for that time I knew why I was being sent!

E. STANLEY JONES:

And yet her simple humility shines through it all. She writes: "It tickles me to see how God uses such big words when He talks to you such as reticence, and how small they are when He talks to me. Golly, He never talks to me like that! But He sure 'lays it on the line' with me just as He does with you. I love Him for that."

This simplicity amid profundity shines out in these final "stories." One day Mary sat down in a train beside a man who was a fatalist.

I began to tell him what I believed in, and he sat up and said to me, "How old are you?" I said: "Thirty-five." He looked at me and said: "Why, I thought you were a high-school kid until I heard that philosophy of yours. That's the most amazing thing I ever heard."

Well, we were real quiet for quite a while, and finally he said: "Would you mind going over that again? I never heard anyone talk or think like you, and it's hard to digest." I said "Why, it's the simplest thing in the world. It would have to be if I got it." He replied, "That's just it. It's too darn simple for me."

Her simplicity and spontaneity are sometimes disconcerting. She sat listening in a church to a very liberal speaker who said that Jesus was dead and that there was no resurrection. Mary was on the edge of her seat listening, and forgetting where she was, she broke out, "Oh, no, you're wrong. He's alive. I was talking with Him this morning!" Those who knew Mary knew it was true! She had been talking with Him that morning, and the radiance of that conversation lingered upon her face.

The simplicity of relationship which Mary has with God is seen in the way He talks with her and she with Him.

The simplicity of relationship which Mary has with God is seen in the way He talks with her and she with Him. After a day in which she had made some difficult decisions and come through with what she calls her "V" for victory, she heard Him say to her as she lay down to sleep: "Sleep well, little one. I love you. Good night." And she adds, "Jesus' love simply breaks me up. It melts me. Gee, how I love Him!"

Mary sums up her life with these words:

"The beautiful part of it all is that every single moment of these years of being a Christian have been so packed with joy and happiness and pure unmerited glory that if all the rest of my life were nothing but trouble and sorrow, I could honestly say to anyone that I've had more than enough blessing to last me all through eternity."

Mary is not a lone star, aloof and unique; she is an example of ordinary human nature extraordinarily responding to grace.

E. Stanley Jones and Mary Webster in c.1958

Mary Webster in 1970s

4

THE MESSAGE

OF

MARY WEBSTER

WITH INTRODUCTIONS

BY

ANNE MATHEWS-YOUNES

One

When I received the Holy Spirit Even the Chickens Knew I was Different

INTRODUCTION

Mary shares a dramatic rendering of her conversion experience, at times both amusing and touching, as we witness the power of God's grace in transforming a life. Her stories are unique and illustrate her narrative gift for describing the main character in her life, Jesus Christ. The reader can scarcely imagine what will come next and where it will all end; even her chickens confirm her changed life....

Even my chickens knew that I had met Jesus Christ because before I became a Christian I hated those chickens. I was a city girl and chickens have mites all over them and they would peck the life out of me. Every time I'd go to get the eggs and reach in the chicken coop, they'd peck me. I got real good at grabbing them by the neck and throwing them off the nest before they could get me. That is the way that I gathered the eggs each day and rather than say thank you for their hard day's work, I'd wring their necks. My chickens hated me. They would see me coming, it seemed like they'd nudge each other, say, "Here she comes, girls. Let's let her have it." I mean, they'd get their beaks ready to go after me. I just hated to go in that hen house. I sure didn't like to go out and get the eggs.

The day after I met Jesus I took the egg basket and I went out to collect the eggs and I realized that the way I treated those hens was me just picking on them. They couldn't talk back to me. So this day I did something quite different. I knocked on the door of the hen house and I said, "Girls, I'm coming in but please don't peck at me because I'm not the same person. Give me a chance." I went in and got down on my knees to pet them and to tell them that I'd never wring their necks again, and from now on I was going to dedicate the earnings from their eggs to the mission field. The old girls just stood up and ruffled their feathers and seemed to say, "Well, help yourself, we love you if you come in this way."

We will also read that the presence of the Holy Spirit is more than rabbit tracks in the snow. Rabbit tracks are no indication of the depth of the presence of the Holy Spirit that Mary was seeking. She was not seeking just a trail of Holy Spirit tracks but the indwelling of the presence of the Holy Spirit in her life.

Without the presence of the Holy Spirit, Mary realizes that she has been in "sales" trying to sell the idea of God instead of letting the Holy Spirit do the work of conversion. She is deeply frustrated by her ineffectiveness as her old stubbornness and anger reassert themselves. Words from E. Stanley Jones and others describing the experience of the Holy Spirit do not help and do not lift her spirits. However, Mary remains open to God's presence and listens. Listening to God will make all of the difference for Mary and can for us as well.

Mary introduces a story about rhubarb pie that will reappear in her next talk. It is well worth reading twice to experience her exceptional storytelling skills and her Jesus-focused message.

Her talk concludes with a description of how she "finally" received the presence of the Holy Spirit. The process by which the Holy Spirit entered her life was initially confusing: was it a vague presence or would it be accompanied by great fanfare? Mary was not interested in drama and, indeed, was afraid of falling prey to some chaotic occurrence. Remember, Mary is at her core, practical and down to earth. She knew that God would pace her spiritual growth but she did feel that something was missing. Below is a glimpse of what happened....

Brother Stanley sent me to a friend who knew all about the Holy Spirit. I agreed to meet with her and said, "Now Selena, I love you very much and I trust your judgment. Brother Stanley told me this afternoon that I had a spiritual need. Do you think so?" You know, I was so sure she'd say, "Why no, Honey, you've got everything you can get."

The funny thing about it was her face just lit up and she said, "Honey, I've been praying for this day." That didn't make me feel too good either, and I said, "Well Selena, Brother Stanley is telling me I need something. What do I need? I love people, and I witness for Jesus, and I love Him. What more could I need?"

Selena continued, "Well Honey, let me put it this way. When I make baking powder biscuits I dump all the ingredients in a bowl and mix them, then I roll the biscuits out, cut them and put them on baking sheets and stick them in the oven. Now, the recipe says, 'Bake for 15 minutes.' If I open the oven door at the end of ten minutes, those biscuits are all golden brown on the outside, but they are not baked in the middle. Honey, there no question that you are in the oven, but you are not baked yet."

Mary would not need to tell Selena when she was fully baked. Read on!

TEN YEARS AGO, on the 19th day of March, in 1950, I was a pretty miserable person, only I didn't know that I was. I went into the Methodist Church in my home town in Illinois and sat down in the third row, and if you've ever been in a Methodist Church you know that nobody's is going to sit in front of you if you go that far down front, and that day I heard Dr. E. Stanley Jones for the first time. He made this amazing statement. He said that it was fun to be a Christian.

I thought that was probably impossible and I certainly didn't know that it was fun. Brother Stanley showed us in his sermon that the reason it was hard for me and fun for him was that I was trying to act like a Christian, but he really was one! Somehow through the Grace of God that night, I gave my heart to Jesus and really fell in love with him in a way that changed me. I thought that Jesus Christ was going to change my family relationships, which Brother Stanley guaranteed. I thought it was about time that the Lord started changing those relationships... and if he'd just make my family appreciate me more we would have it all made! The funny thing was that God didn't touch my family, he just made me appreciate them. The only person he touched was me!

My husband Roy was a farmer and he had to get up early in the morning. Every morning when the alarm would go off at 4:30 I'd lie in bed and think how lucky I was that I didn't have to get him breakfast, rather, he would make mine. After the night I met Jesus, when the alarm went off the next morning I realized that I wasn't lucky, I was just too lazy to get up and do what I should have been doing all along as Roy's wife. So I got out of bed and I went downstairs and made him breakfast. When he came in the kitchen from the barn, the shock of a breakfast prepared by me nearly "killed" him. It was the first time in our married life he'd ever seen me at the breakfast table, and happy at that. Two days later he was talking about miracles with the attendant of the gas station near our house. The attendant said that he didn't believe in miracles. My husband said, "I don't either, but the Lord got my wife making my breakfast and that's miracle enough for me. He doesn't have to change water into wine to demonstrate a miracle."

> **"Live your Christian life and don't say anything about it. At some point, they're going to ask you what's happening, and that's the time I want you to tell them."**

I wanted to witness to my husband and show him that I was a Christian and that I had met Jesus, but Brother Stanley advised against it. He said, "Don't go home and tell people that you've become a Christian. Go home and show them that you have become one. Present yourself. Just live it. Live your Christian life and don't say anything about it. At some point, they're going to ask you what's happening, and that's the time I want you to tell them."

The next day at dinner my little boy came and spilled a glass of milk all over the table. The day before I'd have called him out and given him a lecture and scolded him and felt sorry for myself. But that day, I thought about Jesus and considered that when my little boy spills a glass of milk, a perfectly normal thing for a child to do, that I don't have to get all upset and excited. I got a dishcloth, wiped up the milk, kissed my little son on the head, and thanked God that I was able to offer a Christian response. My little boy looked up at me and he said, "Gee Mommy, what's got into you?" I said, "Just the love of Jesus." He said, "Oh, I like you this way. You used to be like the old witch in the books. You were always mad." I kind of liked myself. It was so much nicer living with a "new" me than getting mad and having a fit.

My sister-in-law lived with us as she had been living with my husband before we married. So, our home had initially been her home. While it may have been her home, it was my house. I didn't really mind her living with me if I could just be the boss. However, she had been the "house boss" for ages and my husband still asked her opinion about everything to do with the house. After a while I began to resent it. I thought, "If I could only find a good way to move her over and let me be boss, then she can live here with me. I just want to give the orders and be the big shot." My sister-in-law wasn't any more Christian than I was and she had no intention of turning that house over to me. She'd worked too hard to get that far and become a homeowner. It was her home and she was going to keep that "ownership" intact.

A sort of cold war began between the two of us. The kind of war that only women know how to fight, where the blood flows, but on the inside, so that no one else notices. But the blood did flow and I starting to do everything that she didn't want done. I did that just to fight with her. For example, I'd go to the store and buy just the opposite kind of food that she liked. I would only buy what I liked.

Then we got to fighting over the window shades. I wanted them up just because she wanted them down. She said the sun would fade the rug. I didn't care about the rug, I was going to have those shades up even if it killed me. Every morning the first thing I'd do is put those shades up, clear to the top, and first thing she'd do is pull them all the way down. I'd put them all up and she'd pull them down. We nearly wore those shades out trying to prove who was boss. There was something inside of me that made me do it. I didn't want to. I knew it was wrong. It made me miserable and it made my husband annoyed.

The first morning after I became a Christian I went to the window to pull the shade up, and just then she walked into the room and something happened to me. The love of Jesus just flooded me and all of the sudden pulling up the window shade to get my own way wasn't the most important thing in the world. Rather to make peace and friends with the woman who brought my husband up and loved him from a little boy and contributed to the character of that wonderful husband was suddenly more important. I went over to her and I asked her to forgive me for being the kind of person I had been and fussing another "shades." I told her that if she'd would pray for me maybe we could change me. She said, "Well honey, if you want the shades up, just put them up, I don't care."

Even my chickens knew that I had met Jesus Christ because before I became a Christian I hated those chickens. I was a city girl and they had mites all over them and they'd peck the life out of me. Every time I'd go to get the eggs and reach in, they'd peck me. I got real good at grabbing them by the neck and throwing them off the nest before they got a hold of me. That's the way I gathered the eggs and rather than say thank you for their hard day's "egg" work, I would wring their necks. My chickens hated me. They saw me coming and it seemed like they'd nudge each other and say, "Here she comes, girls. Let's let her have it." I mean, they'd get their old beaks ready to go after me. I just hated to go in that hen house. I sure didn't like to go out and get the eggs.

The day after I met Jesus I took the egg basket and went out and realized that the way I treated those hens was just me picking on them. I knocked on the door of the hen house and I said, "Girls, I'm coming in but don't peck me because I'm not the same person. Give me a chance." I went in and got down on my knees and pet them and told them that I'd never wring their necks again, and from now on I was going to dedicate the earnings from their eggs to the mission field. The old girls just stood up and ruffled their feathers and seemed to say, "Well, help yourself. We love you if you come in this way."

I began to believe that the scriptures were true. If I had an enemy, I was to love that enemy. Jesus said to love your enemies. That seemed to be the hardest thing I could think of to do and so if I could love an enemy, I might become a good Christian. So I picked out my worst enemy and began to try to love her.

I don't know why this woman didn't like me but she didn't, and every time she saw me she'd just get angry. I decided to try out that scripture about loving our enemies on her. If I couldn't make her love me then I wouldn't believe that scripture. I walked up to her on the street one day and I said hello to her in a very firm but sort of friendly way, since I didn't really like her very much. She just turned her head as if I weren't there and that made me mad. I thought, "Boy, if I weren't a Christian I'd say something nasty to her." I prayed about it and I said, "Lord, why doesn't she love me? I've loved her, now why doesn't she love me?" The Lord said, "Well, try it again."

The next time I saw her I gave her another opportunity. This second encounter didn't work either. However this time, she looked sad rather than mad when I spoke to her. That made me feel badly. So, I prayed again. I said, "Lord, what's the matter? Why doesn't this work?" He said, "Well, Mary, you're asking me to change her. I

Love is the only way to get rid of enemies. Make friends with them. I was amazed at the simplicity of the Gospel message because I thought it was going to be so complex and difficult.

can't. She doesn't want to change, but I can change you and that will help." I said, "Well Lord, there must be something wrong with me that every time that woman sees me I irritate her. Can you help me understand what that irritant is and take it away. I don't want to make her mad every time she sees me."

For two months I prayed day and night that whatever was wrong with me, that made people react negatively to me, that God would somehow show me what it was and remove it. After two months, with one embarrassment after another, this woman, by the grace of God, took me in her arms one morning and kissed me. I don't know why she did that and I didn't even care. I knew one thing, that Jesus didn't tell me to love my enemy because it was hard, but to love them because it worked. Love is the only way to get rid of enemies. Make friends with them. I was amazed at the simplicity of the Gospel message because I thought it was going to be so complex and difficult. However, not to love our enemies is even harder.

I began to experiment with the Bible and while I didn't really understand its truths, I decided to try them out and so I tried them in my "personal laboratory" to see if they worked. And they worked, and soon I began to discover the joy of being Christian. I now know what Brother Stanley meant by using the word "fun" to describe his Christian experience. Since I began to live the life of a Christian instead of that of a wolf in sheep's clothing, I began to have "fun" in the Kingdom. I found out that the love Jesus offers makes it possible for me to love even my worst enemy and to be kind to them. My plan was now to tell others about Jesus and share how wonderful (and fun) it is to be a Christian.

So I discovered that we shouldn't seek God for any special experience but to just love Him and love Him for Himself. Sometimes I feel like the woman who went around with a lamp in one hand and a bucket of water in the other. When someone asked her what she was doing, she said, "I'm trying to burn up Heaven and put out the fires of Hell, so that people will want God for Himself, instead of as a reward or because they're scared." I say this so you won't have any anxiety about trying to secure a particular experience or feeling about Jesus. All you need to do is to give your heart to Jesus Christ, to open up and ask Him to come in, and whether you feel it or not, He's there.

This morning Brother Stanley spoke on the Holy Spirit and that is what I'm going to talk about tonight, only I'm going to let the Holy Spirit speak through me and share with you how this particular experience of grace came into my life almost unsought.

When I was born again, I experienced a tremendous love for Jesus. However, when I was converted, I had no dramatic visions or feelings. That was probably a good thing as it would have scared me to death at that stage of my spiritual growth to see a vision. I didn't need a vision. I didn't need to hear a voice. I just needed to meet Jesus and go home and live with Christ in me. God always gives us what we need spiritually. No more, no less. I say this because some of you might say, "Well, if I only had an experience like yours." Well, my friend, we can't have one another's experiences because we don't need one another's experiences. We all just need the Lord. However He manifests himself to us, it will be according to our unique need. Our experience will be better than anyone else's because it's ours and was designed just for us. All you need to do is give your heart to Jesus Christ. Open up and ask him to come in. Whether you feel it or not, he's there and available to you.

After I had been a Christian for four years, I found that as I looked back on those years, by the grace of God, I lived a gloriously happy life. The Lord left me on a farm for two and half years until he could train me and teach me what I needed to learn to become his witness. The only Christian I knew was Jesus Christ. I had no one to run to when I got in trouble. I had to go to Jesus. I had to get down on my knees right where I was and pray for grace and power and faith. Somehow Jesus seemed to meet me every time I bent the knee to him. He was always there at the moment when I needed him most.

I told you previously that fifteen months after I became a Christian, my family had a terrible car accident in which my husband Roy was killed. I want to share with you how Jesus gave me a tremendous victory and provided support so that I was able to handle this loss. I kept my eyes on Jesus and he saved me from the devastating effects of incapacitating grief. Jesus kept me from having this tragedy destroy me. Thereafter, for four years I was neither up nor down. I was just balanced. I was a perfectly normal and happy person. I managed to get through Roy's death and it really seemed that I got through everything. However, I began to wonder why the Holy Spirit didn't come to me. I read in the Book of Acts that they tarried for so many days, (before the spirit came) and so I thought, "Well, perhaps I haven't tarried long enough."

I asked a good friend of mine, "Why can't I get baptized in the Holy Spirit, or is that just for the people in the Book of Acts?" This man didn't know any more about it than I did and he comforted me like we always do when we don't have anything else to give people. We give them a handkerchief and cry with them. If we don't have faith enough to answer their questions, we just cry with them. I knew that he was trying to make me feel better and while he did not cry with me he said, "Well now, Mary, if you have your garden covered with snow, and if when you wake up in the morning you see rabbit tracks all over the garden, whether you see the rabbit or not, you know he's been there. You can see his tracks." He said, "Now, if you have the fruits of the spirit: love, joy, peace..." He stopped at those three. He continued, "Don't worry about the Holy Spirit. You couldn't have the fruits if you didn't have the spirit."

That relieved a great tension in me. I didn't think much more about it, only his comment about rabbit tracks really didn't seem to satisfy me. I kept wondering but I didn't talk with anyone about my lingering questions.

I didn't need a vision. I didn't need to hear a voice. I just needed to meet Jesus and go home and live with Christ in me. God always gives us what we need spiritually.

Then I began to see something was happening in me. For example, I had an experience with a friend of mine, Jane, and since I had now been a Christian for four years, I was trying to lead her into a conversion experience. I was trying to convince her and sell her on the idea of Jesus. It wasn't God taking hold of her life and converting her, it was me selling her on the idea of Christianity not the reality of Jesus. I was trying to persuade her into conversion. However, all I did was get her so emotionally connected to me that I couldn't get rid of her. She would come to visit, even when I really didn't want her around, and tell me that "Well you've got to take me in because you are a Christian." I began to resent her.

One day she came to our house for the weekend, and I wasn't too happy about it because all she did was give me credit for everything good that happened to her. That habit was becoming annoying. One morning she started telling my sister-in-law, Aunt May, the story about her mother and that she had died, several years ago, Jane told the whole story. I knew it better than she did because it was the only thing she ever talked about. She started with her mother dying and went on and on about it and how much she loved the rhubarb pie that her mother made. She then asked Aunt May to make her a rhubarb pie.

That afternoon Aunt May made the pie and as we sat together to eat it, I remember feeling radiantly happy and victorious and oh how I felt so victorious. Every time Jane told me her troubles, I'd say, "Well keep your eyes on Jesus." Which meant absolutely nothing to her because she couldn't see Jesus. I cut her a piece of pie and pulled up my chair next to her. She then said just three words to me, "Where's your piece?"

Just like that, I don't know how it happened, but she brought up out of my subconscious mind something that had been buried there since I was a little girl. My mother died when I was a baby and I was forced to live with relatives who were alcoholics. The one thing that these people consistently did was to boss me around all the time. They told me when to go to bed and when to get up, and what to wear, what to do, and what to say. The worst thing they did was to make me eat every single food item that they knew I didn't like. The food that I hated the most was rhubarb. They didn't put any sugar in it and seemed to delight in watching me strangle on that horrible stuff. I recall that tons of resentment went into me with every spoonful of rhubarb. I remember saying to myself, "Well there will come a day. I can't do anything about it now, but there will come a day when nobody's going to tell me what to do," and I meant it. I had forgotten all about that for I had met Jesus and I was having such a glorious time with him, even helping winning people to God. However, when Jane asked me where my piece of pie was, all I could see was big Aunt Frances, she weighed 210 pounds, standing over me saying, "Eat that." I forgot all about Jesus Christ and everything. It was just like waving a red flag in front of a bull, and I began to get mad.

I tried to control myself and I said, "Well, I don't care for it," with emphasis on the word *care*, Jane said, "What? You don't care for it?" I said, "No, I don't like rhubarb," with emphasis on the word *like*. She said, "You don't like rhubarb?" I said, "No, I don't like rhubarb. What's so funny about that?" She said, "Taste it, Mary, it's perfectly delicious." I said, "Well you eat it then, but I don't like it and I don't have to taste it. I don't like it." I began to get mad. I wasn't mad at her. She then said to me, "Well gee whiz, I can't imagine anybody not liking rhubarb."

My sister-in-law was at the stove. She had her back to me and she did the most dangerous thing a person can ever do. She put her two cents worth in unasked. She said to Jane, "Mary never eats anything she doesn't like." Boy, I just felt like if I weren't a Christian I'd just hit her. What did she say that for? Then I began to wonder. Has she been thinking about this all this time? Is there an undercurrent here that I'm not aware of? I turned on my sister-in-law and I said, "Well you don't like meringue."

She said, "No, I don't like meringue. I can't bear it." I said, "Well I don't like rhubarb and I can't bear it either. The day you start eating meringue you'll have a right to tell me to eat rhubarb." My girl friend looked at me and said, "Well, you don't have to jump on Aunt May like that. What kind of a Christian are you, anyway?"

Boy, that did it. When anybody throws your Christianity up to you especially when you're feeling angry or unsettled, that is just not fair. I kept saying, "Well, what's Christianity got to do with it? I don't like rhubarb and if you like it, eat it and shut up about it. I don't want to hear any more about it." You know, my conscience, bless its heart, it kept saying, "Mary, Mary, Mary!" I kept saying to my conscience, "Shut up. Don't you get into this." I didn't want my conscience either telling me what to do.

That night I went to bed and I "got over" it. I became aloof and "rose" above it, but I was still mad. I thought that they had no business to start something and just leave me looking like I was in the wrong. I went to bed and I found what Jesus meant when he said that if you have anything against your brother or your sister, before you come to the altar and talk to Him, you better go and make peace with your brother or sister. If you're mad at somebody you can't commune with God. You just can't. I don't know how it happened, but I couldn't get to God. I didn't even care if I talked to God. I thought, "Well it's all his fault. Why doesn't he do something to them? Why doesn't he change them? Why does he let them get away with this?"

I went to bed that night and for the first time in four years, I did not talk to God. You know what happens when you let a resentment go down into your subconscious mind? It begins to grow and it replicates almost as fast as rabbits. By the next morning I was angrier than ever. I kept talking to myself and saying, "Well they shouldn't have started this and that's all right, I don't have to eat rhubarb and nobody's going to make me." I gave myself a big pep talk, but all I could think about was rhubarb.

I went two days and two nights without talking to God and continued to obsess about my predicament and on the third morning the Lord woke me up and said, "Mary, aren't you kind of lonesome out there on that limb you've got yourself on?" I said, "Well Lord, I may be stubborn, but I'm not a hypocrite and I'm not going to say I'm sorry for something that's not even my fault." I continued, "If anything, it's your fault. You made my taste buds different than other people." The Lord said, "Well Mary, you don't even see what's at stake here, do you? You're blind. You don't

> **There is one thing about Jesus... when he puts his light upon a situation he shows you the sin. You can't kid him out of it. He won't let you.**

even see the issue involved. It has nothing to do with rhubarb. It isn't rhubarb pie that you hate to eat. It's humble pie. Rhubarb is simply a symbol of the source of your conflict. You don't like people telling you anything or telling you what to do. When you hear "rhubarb" it brings up in you this un-surrendered part of you that doesn't want to be discovered. Now that it's in the light, what are you going to do about it?"

There is one thing about Jesus... when he puts his light upon a situation, he shows you the sin. You can't kid him out of it. He won't let you. He kept the light there and kept it there until He broke me. I got down on my knees and asked him for forgiveness. I said, "Lord Jesus, if my not liking rhubarb is going to stand in the way of somebody's salvation, Lord I'm going to eat that stuff if it kills me." I thought now, subconsciously, well I'll be so big I'll go out and kill them with kindness. I was secretly hoping it would kill them a little. I thought, "Why don't they come and apologize to me? What is the Lord picking on me for?" I thought, "All right, I'll be the big person. I'll go down to the kitchen, I'll be the heroine and I'll eat this stuff. I'll overcome this impasse with love."

I then told my sister-in-law, "I'm sorry. I've been acting like a perfect fool, just like a two year old." I said to my friend, "Please forgive me if you can, but don't blame Jesus for the way I am. This isn't the way he acts." I said, "I'm going to show you that I'm really sorry, because I'm going to eat this rhubarb. I don't like it, but maybe I would like it if I tried it now. I'm going to eat it."

I dished up this bowl of rhubarb and I put a big spoonful in my mouth and it tasted even worse than I thought it would. I swallowed the stuff. It was just slimy and icky and was awful. I ate spoonful after spoonful. My aunt and friend did not say a word. They were suffering more than I was. After I got through eating, I thought to myself, "Well, I killed you with kindness. I hope you learned the lesson about what it means to be a Christian."

As I put my spoon down, the Lord said to me, "Well, you got off of the 'duty' level, now what about the 'privilege' level? What about a second helping?" I said, "Oh no, Lord. Not another dish." He said, "Well, if you want to be healed you're going have to do this one for free." I found myself dishing up another bowl of that icky, slimy, green, sour rhubarb. I can truthfully say that I didn't like it at all, but I'd eat anything for Jesus. I learned something through this experience. I realized that I often wanted to blame something on someone. But, you know Jesus, he isn't going to let you blame things on your past. He's not going to let you blame it on some infirmity of your flesh or your nerves. He's just going to call your actions or thoughts "sin" and ask you to pray to be forgiven.

Sometime later, (and I assure you that this new topic is related to rhubarb) I learned that I had a cyst that would need to be removed and I was a bit worried. At that time, I was at an Ashram in New Hampshire and they were holding a healing service. Inwardly, I did not believe in healing miracles. I thought that if I asked God to heal me and he did, I would lose respect for God, because he was doing what I told him to do instead of me doing what he told me to do. Well, it's like asking God for a raise when you're not earning what you're getting. I thought, "Well, I do want him to heal me, but then again, I don't want him to heal me. I'm afraid I'll lose my faith if he heals me. Because I don't believe he can do this and I don't really see why he should."

I went to the altar rail and the pastors laid hands on me and prayed. I didn't believe that anything would happen and nothing did. I felt just as sick afterwards as I told before I knelt at the altar. However, I had a feeling of inward relief that the healing did not happen at the service. When I went back to the doctor he advised me to have the cyst removed immediately as it might be malignant.

Instead of following the doctor's advice, I went to another Ashram in Texas. When I got there I learned that there had been a mix up with logistics and the anticipated

Bible teacher could not come. They asked me to take her place and just talk about Jesus. I said, "Sure, I can do that for an hour. You just tell me when to start and when to stop and I'll do it."

At one of the Ashram meetings Brother Stanley spoke on the Holy Spirit. As I listened, I became more and more confused. I didn't understand what he was talking about and I felt sure there were others who were just as mixed up as I was, so I thought, "Well, that's all right. When I get up in the morning I'll explain it to them. I'll tell them all about the Holy Spirit using the rabbit tracks story and set their minds at ease."

So the next morning, I told the group what my friend had told me about the rabbit tracks in the snow. Well, for those who didn't know any better than I did, that illustration seemed to satisfy them. For those who knew better, I could see this look of confusion come into their face, and I didn't know exactly how to take that.

I went swimming later that afternoon and I was having a perfectly marvelous time, and on the way back I ran into Brother Stanley. He said to me, "Young lady, I'd like to have a conference with you." All the sudden something rose up in within me and I thought to myself, "Now what have I done?"

I went to the meeting with Brother Stanley and inwardly I had my dukes up. Brother Stanley said, "I'd like to talk to you about the Holy Spirit." Impulsively I said, "Well if I don't have the Holy Spirit, who's spirit have I got?" He said, "Well, don't make that mistake, Mary. You do have the Holy Spirit, for no one can say Jesus is Lord except by the Holy Spirit. The trouble is, the Holy Spirit doesn't have you. You have to surrender to him just like you did to Jesus." Well, I thought the Holy Spirit was just related to the terminology of the trinity, or was some sort of "influence." I didn't understand at all what he was talking about. Brother Stanley said, "Well don't argue about it. Just kneel down here and ask God to tell you."

I was afraid to ask God. I didn't really know what Brother Stanley was talking about, and a memory flashed into my mind. When I was a little child, I think I was about seven, I went to a Holy Spirit convention. I remember seeing this older woman in the church who was frothing at the mouth and her eyes were fixed in a glassy stare. I said to somebody, "What's the matter with her?" They said, "She's a Saint." I made up my mind right then I would never be a Saint. I had this idea that if anybody was filled with the Holy Spirit, they would be like that and I certainly didn't want God to put a black sun bonnet on me and long stockings and send me out to who knows where.

> **Now Jesus, I don't know what this is all about, but I'm not going to go backwards.**

I had this deep fear about the Holy Spirit. Brother Stanley continued to try to help me. He said, "Mary, it's just wonderful for you to be on the level that you are. God is using you effectively. I want to help you to get from this current level to this new level, but I don't seem to be able to do it." He asked me to go to the chapel to pray so I did.

I knelt in prayer and said, "Now Jesus, I don't know what this is all about, but I'm not going to go backwards. I know that for four years a power that isn't my own has been working through me, giving me victory over so many things. This power has taken me through the death of Roy and made me happy and joyous and radiant and even victorious. This power has been available to me to help me to win people for you. I don't really understand what I need, Lord, but I'm not going to lose what I already have."

I knew that I didn't have what I needed. There was something missing and I lacked something. I know I did. However, because I couldn't understand it intellectually, I thought, "Well I'll let go of it. I'll just let God take care of this "problem." If his plan is salvation, let him worry about it."

Later that afternoon I ran into Brother Stanley again and I said, "You've got to help me. You got me into this mess, now you've got to help me out." He tried to brush me off and as it seemed that he didn't really know what to say to me. I said, "Well Brother Stanley, are you sure you know what you're talking about? Because it's so hard for you to explain all things to me. You're mixing me up." He said, "Well Mary, don't struggle with it. I'm sorry I even raised the question if it's going to upset you like this."

Well, you know, sometimes this is the sort of trouble that can occur when we're too comfortable as Christians. Watch it when you get too comfortable because you're not growing when everything's going too good. You grow best when difficulties are present and you need Jesus. At that point get on your knees and ask for his presence to be with you. You've got to be "upset" once in a while in order for God to keep you growing.

Just then an African American friend of mine went by. She's a minister's wife from Arkansas and she's like my spiritual mother. I have great confidence in her. She is a totally committed Christian who goes around saying, "Glory, Praise the Lord, and Hallelujah." She is like a living dynamo. When you get near her you feel her energy. I didn't have that kind of powerful energy. When she spoke, the things that came out of her mouth were full of graceful power. That was not me.

Brother Stanley to me, "Mary, she knows what I'm talking about. Go and talk to her." I agreed to do so and so I sat down and said, "Now Selena, I love you very much and I trust your judgment. Brother Stanley told me this afternoon that I had a spiritual need. Do you think so?" You know, I was so sure she'd say, "Why no, Honey, you've got everything you can get."

The funny thing about it was her face just lit up and she said, "Honey, I've been praying for this day." That didn't make me feel too good either, and so I said, "Well Selena, he's telling me I need something. What do I need? I'm not full of race prejudice, and I love people, and I witness for Jesus, and I love him. What more could I need?"

She said, "Well Honey, let me put it this way." "When I make baking powder biscuits I dump all the ingredients in a bowl and mix them, then I roll the biscuits out, cut them out and put them on baking sheets and stick them in the oven. Now, the recipe says, 'Bake them 15 minutes.' If I open the oven door at the end of ten minutes, those biscuits are all golden brown on the outside, but they are not baked in the middle." She said, "Honey, there no question you are in the oven, but you are not baked yet."

I know now that she was talking about the message of Romans, but she explained in a way that I could understand. God only ministers to us in the place and in the realm that we're open to and that we can understand. He couldn't come in through intellectual knowledge because I didn't have it. He had to come in through the baking powder biscuits story. I did know something about baking biscuits. The moment she said that, I knew exactly what was wrong with me.

I said, "Look, Selena, when this happens to me, when I am fully baked, will you tell me?" She said, "I won't need to. You'll tell me." I said, "Now listen Selena, I don't want to push God, and I don't want to go off on some mystical experience and be strange. I want to be a normal woman. I want to love my enemies. I want to do the things that are hard to do right here on earth. I don't want God to take me up to some seventh realm of Heaven and tell me a lot of things that will make me different from other people." She said, "Don't you worry. You just stay open." She then said, "Mary, you are just like a little child who is going to God and stamping your foot and saying, 'Talk to me.'" "Shut up and listen, Honey, he's talking to you." So she made me get perfectly quiet. Then I thought, "All right, Lord, I don't know what I need. I don't know what you call it. I don't know what works best, but here I am. I'm going to bed tonight and you worry about it."

I surrendered it and went to bed. In the night, I had a feeling of expectancy and a deep, urgent feeling came up within me and I woke very early the next morning. I took a shower and I put on the best dress that I had and went off to the communion service. I started to pray. We were having a silent communion service where all of us, all 300 of us, gathered together under one roof with one mind and one spirit, all loving Jesus and talking to him.

I sat at the very back of the auditorium because I didn't want to bother anybody and I didn't want anybody to be around me in case I started shouting or yelling as I had no idea what would happen to me. I thought, "Well, I want to get far enough away that I won't distract these people and upset the meeting." I knew something was going to happen. I sat there with my eyes closed. I thought, "Well, I don't want people to distract me. I want to look at Jesus. I want to find out what's the matter with me."

I gave up using the words Holy Spirit because I didn't know what to call "him" or "it." I didn't even know what I wanted, so I quit thinking about him. I began to think about my life and how far apart my life was from the life that Jesus lived on earth. All of a sudden the Lord got my attention, and you know if he gets your attention, something can happen.

God only ministers to us in the place and in the realm that we're open to and that we can understand.

As we sat there, they began the Communion service and passed first the bread, then the wine. As I heard the words of the Minister saying the words of Jesus at the Last Supper, "This is my body, broken." I experienced the word "broken" with my ears and I could hear the "snap" of something breaking. "This is my blood," the pastor said and I realized in a flash what had been the matter with me. I said, "Jesus, all these years that I've walked with you, I've been glad it was your body and your blood and not mine that was sacrificed. I was always defending myself and protecting myself. I don't want to die. I want to live. But I can see now what is the matter. I wanted to be with you, but I never dreamed of being like you. To become broken bread and poured out wine. Lord Jesus, when I came to you as a sinner, I offered you many things. You said to me, 'I don't want your gifts. I don't want your money. I don't want your service. I don't want your loyalty. I want you.'"

I said, "Well, I'm coming back to you tonight. Not as a sinner, but as a child of God. I'm yours." I came to God and said, "I want to belong to you, lock, stock, and barrel. I don't want to think a thought that's not from you. I want to be totally and utterly dependent upon you because I choose you. Not because I have to but because I want to be dependent upon you for everything."

With my eyes still closed, I saw a vision, and it was the first time for me to experience a vision. It was of a clear square glass vase. It was completely empty and it was just slowly filling to the top. God was trying to show me what he was doing to me. That the moment I got empty enough of myself, he could fill me. If I was half full of self he could only fill me half full of him. The moment I became the empty manger, he could fill me with the Christ child.

I was so full of the love of God. I wanted to just put my arms around people. I wasn't even thinking about the Holy Spirit. I was just thinking about people and God and how much I loved them both and I wanted to get them together. I thought, "My heart's going to break right here in front of these people. I can't contain this kind of love." He's just pouring his love through me.

They dismissed us from the communion service and I wanted to get out of there so fast. I thought I just had to get out of the room. I took a hold of a woman who was in my way and I wanted to shove her out of the way and say, "I'm in a hurry." Usually I would have pushed that woman out of the way, excused myself, and gone on to do something spiritual. The moment I touched her, the voice within me said, "But Mary, we don't do that anymore, do we? We don't go around shoving people in order to do something spiritual. We just don't do that anymore, do we?"

Always before the inner voice had said to me, "You can't do that and be a Christian." It was like God walking beside me constantly and advising me. Now it was different, it was like God saying within me, "You and I have the same reputation. We have the same character, the same everything. You and I are one now, so we don't do things like that, do we? We're going to think before we speak. We're going to be kind and loving and patient. We've got all eternity. We

> **Lord Jesus, when I came to you as a sinner, I offered you many things. You said to me, 'I don't want your gifts. I don't want your money. I don't want your service. I don't want your loyalty. I want you.**

don't have to knock people out of the way to do something spiritual. We've got time. You and I together are going to live out your life."

I was so different. I didn't have to push that woman. I just waited. I went to the altar of prayer and I got down and started to kiss his feet. Now, the one thing that I have always wanted more than anything is to wear a Sari like the Indian women do because I've loved India for so long.

Mary Webster wearing a Sari, 1967

It was through my interest in India that I found Jesus. My love of India brought me to the church to hear a missionary from India who turned out to be Brother Stanley. It was through my love for India that I found Jesus.

I've always wanted to wear a Sari. When I was on my knees at that altar, I could just feel like God, my heavenly father, was saying, "Come here, Mary. Come here. You've always wanted to love people. You've always wanted to wear a Sari." He said, "Honey, look at the world. Look at all those broken, bleeding people out there." He said, "You know what I'm going to do? I'm going to answer your prayer. You've always wanted to be a nurse. I'm going to put your uniform on you. I'm going put a Sari of love right around your heart. I'm going to have you love people like you never could have loved them before. I'm going to love people through you. I'm going to make you sensitized, not sensitive, but sensitized to the needs of other people. You're going to hear a broken heart a mile away and you're going to have this wonderful power to run in my name and in my strength to do something for that person."

He said, "Mary, I'm going to put a nurse's cap on you and I'm going to tie on your apron." Then with authority, he said, "Now go out and find us the broken, bleeding hearts of people and tell them about me. That's going to be your vocation from now on."

111

Brother Stanley said this morning that the Holy Spirit converts you but he convicts you first, and he did the conviction with that rhubarb. He converts you as well and he did that for me at the altar. He commissioned me and he wants you. He gave me my occupation and the power to do what he has called me to do. I wasn't going to do it alone, but God was going to do it through me.

I wondered if Brother Stanley would realize that something had happened to me, and I thought, "Well if it's true, if God really has invaded me and come within me, surely Brother Stanley ought to be able to tell without my telling him."

My friends, I learned one of the biggest lessons of my life. It's one thing to be able and want to serve God. However, when you can move over and let somebody else serve God who you might think was not as good at it as you are, but let them help, that is real humility. That is what Brother Stanley did, and he thanked God for using Selena to help me when he couldn't because he was trying to reach me on a level that was not yet available to me.

Selena came to me at my level. Later that afternoon we were in my room praising the Lord. Just like that, at three o clock on the dot, the Lord healed me. I didn't even believe in healing. I didn't even ask him to heal me. I grabbed Selena and I said, "Oh no, Selena. He's healed me. I'm well. I know I'm well and I don't even believe in such healing." She said, "Well Mary, you learned a big secret in the Kingdom. As long as you sought the healing, you didn't get it. However, when you found a healer, you got both — the healing and the healer." She said, "Mary, it's much better for you to have been sick all your life and found a healer, than to have received the healing and missed him."

When I got back home, I went back to my doctor and I told him that I didn't need an operation, I knew I was well and whole. The Lord had healed me. I told my doctor that, "I had major surgery, all right. Not on my body, but on my heart." Well, the doctor, being a medical man and not a Christian, said, "Well now, I've got to examine you," and he did. He said, "Well I don't know. You're right. There isn't any cyst there to operate on." Then he started to tell me in medical terms what had happened to me. He didn't understand me. I didn't understand him, but I knew that Jesus had come. That the Holy Spirit had come within and driven him out. I'm like the girl that Brother Roberto told us about this afternoon. Something started in me that has never stopped.

A few weeks later I was in a Southern woman's home in Texas and she said to me full of anger and in front of a lot of people "Well, I don't want to love everybody in the world," meaning non-White people. She asked me, "Do you?" I said, "No, but ever since this has happened to me, I can't help it. I'm not choosing to love them. God is loving them through me. I'm just an open shaft. I don't even understand it. I'm just letting love go through me."

This is what the Lord wants us to have. The power to live the life that Jesus offers us when we surrender our all. Tonight Brother Stanley said he was going to have an altar call service. He's going to give you an opportunity, not just to seek, but to receive the Holy Spirit. I realize now, as I look in retrospect, that the Lord will not lay the cross upon your shoulders unless you ask him to do so.

This isn't something you receive that makes you better than anybody else. This is the power to learn how to live and you don't get it unless you ask for it. You can go a long way with Jesus Christ.

I had a friend who was a very wonderful singer, and maybe some of you would even know him if I told you his name. He had the most beautiful voice in the world. He came to me one night as he sought the Holy Spirit and said, "Mary, there's only one thing I want in all this world, and that is to sing for Jesus." I said, "Son, are you willing to lay your voice upon the altar and be willing not to sing for Jesus if that would please him more?" "Oh," he said, "Mary, that's my life. What could I do if I couldn't sing for Jesus?" I said, "Well, when you come to the place where you can sing for him or not sing for him according to what he wants, then he'll come. Lay your all upon the altar."

It took that young man a long time to make up his mind, but finally he framed the words and the Spirit of God came within him. The Lord didn't take away his desire to sing, but he knew that the young man could live his life without singing. He was no longer tied up with his vocation at all. Throw your all on the altar tonight and expect the spirit of God to come in. He said he would if we'd ask him. The moment we ask him, he comes. If our heart meets the condition, he will come because he says so.

Shall we pray?

Mary Webster in early 1960s

Mary Webster in 1980s

Two

Making Room for the Holy Spirit to Witness

INTRODUCTION

This talk makes it clear, as we read in the previous one, that while we might think we are doing the work of "witnessing" to others, that is not the case. Mary is now convinced that it is not Mary who is witnessing, (in spite of her deep desire to play that role), rather it is the Holy Spirit witnessing through her. She also realizes that this "fact" is all the more reason to ensure a continued deep connection with the Holy Spirit as the following paragraph conveys.

I was in a restaurant one day talking to a Christian friend of mine about Jesus and the next thing I knew the waitress kept coming to our table. She came when we were having our prayer, and when she came back with the second cup of coffee, she left a note with it. "May I speak to you outside when you are finished?" She had a problem and believed that since we knew the Lord she could talk to us about Him. Now the thing is this, the Holy Spirit really does the witnessing. When God is using you and me the most we know it the least. When you think God is using you the most He is probably is not using you at all. For example, if you are aware of "God using you" then it is you doing the work. But when God is doing the work, you are not even aware of it because God is doing it.

Mary reminds us that in witnessing we should never try to talk to a person about Jesus until you have first talked to Jesus about that person. If you pray first and receive the guidance of the Holy Spirit about what God wants done in that person's life then you may move forward. However, she recommends that we listen intently for sometimes God is telling us to "leave them alone." God treats us gently and Mary reminds us that we should do likewise. Mary illustrates this advice by sharing a story about Jan in which God, not Mary, did all the work.

We really do not have the power to make others see Jesus. Mary believed that you must have the experience of Jesus in order to have something to show and the ability to "see" as Christ's witnesses.

All we do is provide the atmosphere to witness. The Holy Spirit does it. We don't do it. The Holy Spirit does!

OPENING PRAYER

Lord we thank you for Jesus and for the Holy Spirit, and we thank you that we know that you love us in spite of what we are, and even because of what we are, and we pray this morning that would you help us to go into this broken world, and tell people the Good News, that God is having a "come as you are party"and that everyone is invited. We pray God that you will loosen our tongues and have us speak of You instead of the weather or other trivial things we so typically talk about. And give us the consciousness and awareness of your Holy Spirit so that we can't think of anything but you. We ask it all in Jesus name. Amen.

Yesterday, we said that witnessing was the church at work, and if the church is at work, doing God's business the first thing we would do is to be witnessing, because we are His witnesses and that our witness is a window through which others see God. Usually that window is like the jaggedness of stained glass representing our brokenness through which God reveals Himself to us. As we are willing and enabled by the Holy Spirit to reveal to others just how far God has taken us from our broken lives to wholeness, they will begin to see the wonderful works of God revealed.

When we witness, we really don't do it, the Holy Spirit does it through us. I believe that every minister has had the experience that I will now tell you about. When you visit a hospital room you are also witnessing to others. Maybe your care receiver is a member of your congregation, and maybe they are in a hospital room with two or three other patients and so you lower your voice as you talk with your parishioner about God and have fellowship and prayer. However, as you are leaving the room, the person in the third bed, to whom the Holy Spirit was witnessing, calls you aside and says: "Preacher, come over here. I don't have a preacher. I don't have anybody, but I've got to have God." And you find that while you were witnessing to one person, God was witnessing to someone who you didn't even know was listening.

I was in a restaurant one day talking to a Christian friend of mine about Jesus and the next thing I knew the waitress kept coming to our table. She came when we were having our prayer, and when she came again with the second cup of coffee; she left a note with it. "May I speak to you outside when you are finished?" She had a problem and believed that since we knew the Lord she could talk to us about Him. Now the thing is this, the Holy Spirit really does the witnessing. When God is using you and me the most we know it the least. When you think God is using you the most He is probably is not using you at all. For example, if you are aware of "God using you" it then it is you doing the work. But when God is doing the work, you are not even aware of it because God is doing it. This is important to understand.

A friend of mine (and I) went to a campus and saw some large stones out in front of the building all covered with ivy. One section of the ivy had climbed up the wall but a vine had moved off of the anchoring stones into the air and had broken off and was dying. A minister wrote these beautiful words as he saw what had happened to the ivy.

"An ivy vine should never leave a wall of stone, God never fashioned it to climb the heights alone, no more can we by dreams possess to daily plod, reach yearning heights beyond the stars, apart from God."

I see a lot of Christians running ahead of the Holy Spirit, trying to do His work. And it just isn't possible. One woman said to me, 'There is nothing we can do but pray,' when you call in the sum total of the

> **When God is using you and me the most we know it the least. When you think God is using you the most He is probably is not using you at all.**

Universe, to help you out, yes, 'all we can do is pray', and that is the finest thing that we can do.

Another thing that I learned is that you should never try to talk to a person about Jesus until you have first talked to Jesus about that person. If you don't know anything about a person's background, if you don't know anything about a person's problems you violate that person, and that is not Christian. But if you pray first and receive guidance from the Holy Spirit to do what God wants done in that person's life, (and sometimes God is telling you 'leave her alone") then you get the needed direction. God treats us gently, and we should treat others likewise. Jesus

121

stands at the door and knocks, and He doesn't try to come in until we open the door and ask Him to come in.

Another thing to remember in witnessing is that all God asks us to do is to provide an atmosphere in which a person would want to open the door, even a crack…to let the light come in. And that is really not hard to do because we don't have to do anything but just love people, drawing on the love that God puts in our hearts when we are fully surrendered to him. All that love creates a positive atmosphere.

I was talking to a girl (Jan) the other night from a Church of God congregation. If you would ask her Church of God minister if he really preaches the Gospel, he would say 'yes.' And he might believe that if you are not saved in that church it would be your own tough luck. However, because the altar calls are given, and the Gospel is preached, if you don't take up the offer, then it is because you are not ready. Jan told me, "You know my family is Christian. I've been brought up Christian and been taught all the Scriptures and everything. I know it all but I don't believe any of it. I am not a hypocrite, I just don't believe it." So I responded, 'You mean you don't believe in anything?' She said, "No I don't. To me it is all just fantasy." And I continued, 'Well if you were in a tunnel, and you were walking through it with a candle, but all of a sudden a gust of wind blew out your candle, you might became afraid to walk because you would not know if one step in the dark might be your last. However, if I came along behind you with a candle, now that might not be much light but it would be more light than you had. Are you going to be foolish enough to blow out my light too so we both stumble and fall or would you rather follow me with my little light as dim as it is until you could get your own light? She said, "I would rather follow you with your dim light." Well I said, 'darling you are in a tunnel of darkness and doubt. Now I can't really do anything about that, but I can come along with you in that same tunnel with a light, and while it is not much of a light, it is a lot more light than you have."

I continued, "Is there anything in my life at all that would say to you that God is alive?' She said: "Yes, I guess it would be in your smile. You couldn't be that happy if something wasn't kicking inside of you." So I continued 'Well, alright now, I can't give you Jesus

You should never try to talk to a person about Jesus until you have first talked to Jesus about that person.

Christ, and I can't really do anything, but share my light with you, so let's walk out of the tunnel together until we get out into the light. And when you are in the light, God will reveal Jesus to you. God is the only one who can. I can't explain it to you and I can't argue about it with you. There was a time when I thought I could but I have since learned that I can't. But I will pray with you and for you. And we'll pray that God will reveal to you what you want to know about Jesus and if there is any reality to Him. Now if God can't do it, there is no sense in me trying. So I am going to pray a prayer, step by step, and you can repeat my words as long as you can honestly say that you believe what you are saying, but when you come to a place in the prayer where you do not believe it, we'll stop right there. So I began to pray a simple prayer, *Lord I hear you knocking on the door of my heart,* she prayed that, *Lord I want you to come in,* she prayed that, *Lord I sinned against you,* she prayed that, *Lord I am sorry that I did it,* she prayed that, *Lord I accept you as my Savior and Lord,* she said: "I can't say that." I said, 'Okay, then don't.' Then I started to pray; *Lord this girl is in a tunnel.She still in darkness and You are the only one that can turn the light on inside of her. Please show her who Jesus is.* And then I said goodnight to Jan. When I left her, she was in darkness,but that's the place to leave people until the Holy Spirit shows them Jesus.If you try to do it, you violate them. You will give them your impression of who you think Jesus is. And that is not the same as when Jesus shows the person who He is. When you try to get them to trust or believe your perspective that does not work.

I called her up the next day and I said to Jan, 'How are you?' However, I could tell by the tone of her voice that nothing had happened. So I changed the subject but I continued to pray for her. And I called her up at noon – nothing had changed. I continued to pray for her and went to see her a little later in the afternoon — still nothing. I didn't ask her, I didn't push it, I just could tell by looking at her that nothing had happened for her yet...But that night when she came to the church, I didn't have to ask her, I could see. The Lord had come. He had shown her who He was and she had received Him.

I think too often we are trying to make people have this experience of Jesus. We want to make them see Jesus, we really want them to. And God wants it to happen more than we do. However, we can't push it because God doesn't push it. He waited 33 years for me to see the light. But when I saw the light, I saw the Light! Not because man showed it to me, but because God revealed to me who Jesus was. While He did through a man, Brother Stanley, it was really God who did it.

The Scripture this morning is from Luke's gospel, the 11th chapter, where Jesus said these amazing words, "But if it is by the finger of God that I cast out demons, then the Kingdom of God has come upon you." They were calling Him a devil, but Jesus said: "But if I by the finger of God cast out devils, no doubt the kingdom of God is come upon you" (Luke 11:20). That phrase is the most beautiful illustration of what you and I can be to God if we are available to serve as His finger. And why the finger? The finger points to something. And you and I can be God's finger and let Him point people to the Way. We can point them to Jesus. That is what John the Baptist was, a pointer God used to point to the Lamb of God, telling others, "this is it."

Now, I have a picture that somebody gave me and I know many of you have seen it. The picture is pertinent here because it explains this effort of trying to persuade people to see Jesus. That is very foolish thing to do because it never works that way. This is a photograph that was taken of the "ground." A Chinese photographer was riding on his horse one day when he heard about Jesus. He wanted to believe, but he was a Buddhist and he didn't want to do something he shouldn't do, so he said, 'Lord if I can but see your face, I would believe,' and the voice said, 'photograph the ground.' He took a picture of the ground. It was of snow on mud but he took it home and developed it, and out of the snow and mud emerged this beautiful face of Jesus, and you can't mistake who He is. The photographer became a Christian as a result of this

The Ground

experience. Well, this picture is a strange thing. You can't see Jesus when you first look at it. All you see is black and white.

Now the person who showed you the picture must have seen the Lord, or they wouldn't be showing you the picture. That's what I am saying, you have to be able to see Jesus, or you couldn't be a witness. You got to have the experience of Jesus in order to share him. A woman brought me into her studio, and showed me the picture that the Chinese photographer took. I wanted to be able to see the Lord in the picture. And so I tried. I just looked at it. I could see what it looked like and everything, but I could not see Jesus. And then she did the typically helpful thing, she tried to show me. So she showed where his face was, where his hair was, where his eyes were. The eyes didn't look like eyes at all. And I struggled to see them, but I could not as there was nothing for me to see. It was just black and white. The harder she tried to show me that picture, the less I was able to see it. And then because I didn't want to act too stupid, I said, "Yes I see it." She responded, "No you don't, you don't act as if you do see Jesus." And then I thought, I don't know how I am supposed to act but finally I said, 'Ok, I don't see it, and I am not going to try to see Jesus anymore,' and I turned to walk out the door. However, something drew me to look back at the picture once more and there He was. I didn't need somebody to show me, He showed me who He was.

Some time later, after having this experience somebody gave me a similar "illusion" picture, this time one of a cow. The cow was hidden in the picture, and it said underneath it, 'hunt the cow,' and I said, 'if the cow wants

The Cow

me he can hunt me.'I am going to stand right here and let the cow come to me. The cow did not hunt me, but that is what Jesus does. He just appears and you see Him and if you don't see Him then you don't see Him, period. You see the form that somebody showed you but you don't see Him. And I don't want the form. I want the Person. And so it's foolish for us to try to think of ways to convert others. We can't.

You can't take by cesarean section that which has never been conceived by the Holy Spirit. Until the Holy Spirit starts to work on a person, there is nothing to do. So all Jesus asks us to do is to provide the atmosphere. To provide the atmosphere will take a lifetime because there are a lot of things that the Lord wants to do for others. Many times, just in conversation, we can make people aware of Jesus without even trying to witness.

I was in an airport the other day, waiting to get on a plane and a man came up behind me and I moved aside. (I always let everybody get on the airplane first and then they don't gripe because I took the best seat). I always take the last seat available because I don't care where I sit as long as I arrive. And so this man came up behind me and said, "Hey lady, is there a cigarette machine around here anywhere?" I smiled at him when I said: 'I hope not.'He looked at me in a kind of funny way and so I said: 'Well you look like a rather nice chap and I don't want you to die of lung cancer.' I continued, 'My father died of lung cancer. He smoked for years and couldn't stop, un-til they told him he had lung cancer; then he stopped but it was too late.' I said: 'I wouldn't want that to happen to you.' He said: "Well it will be two hours before this plane lands, before I can have another cigarette." I said: 'Well if you can quit for two hours, you can probably quit forever.' "No, I couldn't," he said. I added, 'Have you prayed about it?' He responded, "How did I get into a conversation like this?" I smiled to myself and thought, well, he just picked the wrong person. Then he saw a vending machine and said, "Well I see a machine down there. I hope I have time to get my cigarettes." I yelled at him, 'I hope it's empty.' I was not intruding on him as he approached me and brought up the subject. I simply was loving him. I saw my dad die from lung cancer and I didn't want anybody to die that way. I often ask myself, why do they

> I think too many times we are trying to make people have this experience of Jesus. We want to make them see Jesus, we really want them to. And God wants it to happen more than we want it to happen. However, we can't push it because God doesn't push it.

put on a package of cigarettes that they won't hurt you? That makes no sense. They don't put that on cornflakes. It is all a trick to sell cigarettes. Well, the man returned and again he approached me and held up the cigarette package and said: "Looks like the Lord let you down. What are you going to say about that?" I continued, "Honey, when you are gasping your last earthly breath, remember, the Lord didn't let me down, you let Him down. He could save you from this if you would let Him." And finally I said, "You know any guy can give up smoking, but it takes a real courageous man to face lung cancer."

We had a carpenter come to our house to do some repair work, and every other word out of his mouth was a curse word because he did not know the Lord. I wanted this man to be converted. I found that I could not stand the swearing and so I went to him and said, "Sir, do you want to know the plan of salvation?" And he said: "Hell no." And I said, "Well I think you do Sir, because I have been listening to what you have been saying, and you say three things consistently, God, Jesus Christ, and hell. You are in hell, you want to get to God, and you have got go through Jesus Christ. That is the plan of salvation. And you keep talking about it all the time, why don't you give in to it?" And the man looked up at me somewhat confused and I continued, "You know you are giving away your case, you are advertising that you are in need, because you are yelling out for the only person who can help you. And I want to help you to find that person." You know he couldn't swear after that because he knew every time he did, that I would be praying for him. He knew he was advertising the fact that he was lost. I didn't have to tell him that he was lost.

Each of us can provide the atmosphere for the Holy Spirit to work. You know when that same guy came to me to bill me, he said: "You know I got a confession to make." And I freeze at this sort of comment because I am not a confessional, and I don't like people dumping their confessions on me. What I always want to tell them is to share their sins with Jesus. He is the "sin collector," I am not. I am the one who brings Him mine. So I said to the carpenter, "Well, take it easy, what is it that you want to confess?" He said: "You know when you hired me, you told me to keep track of my time, and you said you would not have hired me if you didn't trust me to keep track of my own time, oh… and I thought, 'boy is she crazy, I'll really pad this,' and I intended to charge you a $100 extra." (And I would have been too stupid to know the difference.) But he continued, "It's pretty hard to cheat a person who believes you are more honest than you really are and I want you to know that I took $50 off of your bill." Jesus saves! He saved me $50! All you do is provide the atmosphere. The Holy Spirit does it, you don't do it. He does it.

I was recently in an airport at Christmas time and everyone was trying to get somewhere and my flight was over sold. There were about 15 people, including me who were not going to make that flight. Well a guy walked up to the ticket counter and said, "I got a ticket here and I am going to ride on this plane." And the attendant responded, "Well Sir, we are trying to work this thing out. You just have to be patient because we made a mistake, we oversold this flight, we are very sorry." And the traveler yelled, "Jesus Christ." So, I walked up to him and I said, "Sir, He is the only one who can get you on that plane, but not when you talk to Him in that tone of voice." And everybody in the area begin to look at us and I then said to the man, "No kidding, He could help you without hurting any of us, and He will, but not when you talk to Him in that way." And that man looked at me as if to say, "drop dead and get out of my way." He was mad, and turned and then left the area. But as soon as he left, you know what happened? That ticket counter attendant said: "They have just sent me word. We are going to put on a second flight." The guy who left angry because he was not going to listen to anybody would miss the flight. He didn't make that second flight and he could have, as there was plenty of room on that plane, but he was sore. All we can do is to just witness to people and provide the atmosphere.

Here is another idea, when you get into an elevator and if there is anybody in it, when you get off turn around and say to them, 'I hope your last trip is up, not down', and walk away. Let the Holy Spirit work with that one. He will. He will just work on the person. You provide an atmosphere. When you make people realize that they may be lost, they'll come begging to God to be found and be made whole. You don't have to do it. The Holy Spirit does it.

A man said to me one day: "You know, I am so unlucky that if there was only one train going to heaven, and there were three vacant seats, and only two people got on, I still wouldn't make it with my luck." And I said, "Would you say that again?" There must be something in what you say that we can use. He made his comment again. "If there was only one train going to heaven, and three empty seats, and only two people got on, I still wouldn't get on, I still couldn't make it with my luck." I said, "Aren't you glad we are not going by train? We are going by Jesus and we can all make it if we want to." You could see the look of relief come on to his face.

Now we want to remember that after we provide this atmosphere, God will work in the atmosphere, as we keep the atmosphere in a spirit of love. I don't know how many of you know Mary Light. She has this precious little admonition to Christians –'Love, don't shout; Nestle, don't wrestle.'

For example, Mary Light's husband came home one night so mad at the church board meeting... He threw down his shoes and got ready for bed, but continued to gripe to her. When he got into bed she snuggled up to him and said, "What other blessing did you receive tonight, Honey?" And right away the guy began to laugh. Another time, he came home and was so mad at someone and said, "I am going to call the guy and really blast him out." She said, "Well, Honey, let's have a word of prayer first and then you go and tell him off." And he said, "Oh shuss, you know I couldn't do that if I prayed about it." She says, "I know that." Isn't it wonderful to have a wife like that. Amen.

Now in this atmosphere, if God is going to use you as His finger to point the Way, we have got to be out of the Way. We often become a stumbling block, not a stepping-stone. It's our own ego, and our own pride that will get in the way of Jesus. Just like I said when I began this talk, our witness is a window through which others see God. We are the windows, and the finger that God is going to use. Amen!

Mary Webster, E. Stanley Jones and others, 1960s

THREE

THE ROLE

OF

A WITNESS

INTRODUCTION

A witness can serve as the finger of God pointing the way towards Jesus and can also serve as God's mouthpiece. However to be a witness, we must be obedient. We often want to help God so much that we sometimes get in his way instead of simply being available if He needs us. Mary illustrates this point with the following story…

The Bible says something interesting about grass that it doesn't say about anything else. It says that grass grows in the deepest sea, and it grows above the timberline. Grass grows in the highest places and the lowest places on Earth for one reason: grass is obedient to God. It never complains because people walk on it. It never complains because it isn't a tree or that it doesn't have a smell. Grass is just obedient. It just grows where God puts it, so it grows everywhere.

If we could learn this art of surrendering, like the grass, to God, to be just whatever God made us for, just to be that person, that would be the greatest thing in the world. God wrote the drama of life, and he's never miscast a single character. We sometimes just don't want to play the part he gave us because we think that isn't as great a part as someone else might have.

The other important job of a witness is to love, to love God and the people in the world for nothing. Just love them. Mary writes,

Love is a possibility in all of our relationships. I can be a channel of love through which God can work, but sometimes I am not such a channel. Every time I am not such a channel I hurt a person, which really means that I hurt Jesus. That's why I come to Christian Ashrams, and that's why I ask you to pray for me. I want to continue to be a channel of love.

Mary shares her many lessons in humility and in particular her growing capacity to say, "I am sorry. I was in the wrong."

Isn't it wonderful that God gives you the power to say, "I'm sorry. I'm wrong." He gives us that power when we're really sorry. Our greatest witness comes when we're willing to go back and tell somebody that we were in error.

Mary closes her message with this prayer:

> Father, we just love everybody in this room because you love us. You give us the power to love each other. You give us tears to cry, and you give us arms to love, and hands to serve, and feet to do things for people. Help us to make use of these wonderful faculties to show you how much we love you by doing everything we do in your name and in your spirit. Help us in our relationships with our friends. Help us, Father, to witness and become the church at work as we go about our Father's business. We ask it in Jesus' name, Amen.

OPENING PRAYER

> *Father, we thank you this morning that we have something to sing about. We thank you for Jesus who gave us his life that we might have our lives. We pray that we won't just take this life as if it belonged to us, but give it back to God so that he might show us what He made us for and help us to become that person, not to be somebody else but to be whatever He made us to be and be willing to be that person to his glory. We ask it all in Jesus' precious name, Amen.*

I want to say something more about the role of a witness. I have often said that a witness is like a stained glass window through which people can see God. A witness is also like a living bridge over which people walk into the arms of Jesus. Our lives, when we're willing to share them, become a bridge over which people can walk into victory in Christ. A witness can also serve as the finger of God pointing the way to come home to Jesus. And finally, a witness is God's mouthpiece or God's advertising page.

We have been reading Paul's letter to the Corinthians (1 Cor. 13:1-13) and it is often called the "love chapter." I thought it was kind of mean of Paul to use the word "it" as a stand in for the word "love." He writes, "it" does this, and "it does that, and "it's" not this, and "it's" not that. However in one instance, he writes, "Love does not behave un-seemingly and seeketh not her own." Now, I wonder why in this instance did Paul make "it" feminine? I don't insist on my own way; I demand it. From this chapter, I learned the following: love in relation to sin is grace, and love in relation to suffering is mercy. Love in relation to trials and temptation is peace. Love in relation to death is resurrection. If we are going to live a life of God, it's going to be a life of love. It's going to be love in a relationship.

A witness is like a stained glass window through which people can see God. A witness is also like a living bridge over which people walk into the arms of Jesus.

I know a lot of people who love God but who don't love people. It doesn't work that way. The only way I can offer my love to God is through somebody. I remember one time I was in a retreat center with Sister Estelle Carver.[1] She was tired and getting ready to go to Europe. I had some of these soothing eye pads, which when you put on your eyes and lie down for 15 minutes you feel like you slept an hour because they relax all the muscles around your eyes.

I knew Sister Estelle had a heavy schedule and I knew that she was tired. I had learned the art of massage from Sister Leila.[2] I just felt that I should give Sister Estelle a

---

[1] Estelle Carver was a well-known and well-loved Bible teacher at Christian Ashrams in the 1960s

[2] Sister Leila was a Greek Orthodox nun who often traveled with E. Stanley Jones

massage, and place the soothing pads on her eyes – just do it quietly and then leave. You know what the Lord said? Don't do it. If you have a garden and you have a rose blooming in it, you can do one of two things. You can go out with a sharp knife, cut the rose, and bring it into the house so you can enjoy it and smell it. You can do one better thing: leave the rose alone, and then everybody can enjoy it and smell it.

God told me, "If you really love Estelle, don't go and do nice things for Estelle. However, in her name and with love for her, offer these "gifts" to your roommate, a person that nobody ever does anything for. Everybody does things for Sister Estelle. People are falling all over themselves wanting to give her things, buy her things and do things for her. However, no one ever does anything for the roommate that I put you with. Offer your comfort to her in honor of Estelle, and leave Estelle alone."

So, I went over to my roommate and I said, "Are you tired?" She said, "Yes." I said, "I know you're a chiropractor, but I'm a masseuse in the name of the Lord. I want to offer you a back rub. I want to make you comfortable." I began to massage her back and offered her the soothing eye pads and then I prayed for her. She began to cry. She said, "Nobody in the world ever did that for me. I have a lot of patience, but I don't have anybody who has patience with me." I wouldn't have done that for her if God had not told me this little secret. If you love God, show others that you love them. In doing that, God knows you love Him. I left Estelle alone, which is probably the nicest thing I could do for her, and offered my roommate some attention and comfort.

*E. Stanley Jones, Tom Carruth, Estelle Carver
and Mary Webster*

Sister Leila and E. Stanley Jones

141

E. Stanley Jones, Mary Webster and others at Keuka Ashram, 1958

You know when a child comes into the kitchen and says, "Mama, can I help you?" The mother sometimes says, "Yeah, get out of the kitchen." We want to help God so much, that we sometimes get in his way instead of just being available if He needs us. I remember something Brother John said about what the Bible says about grass that it doesn't say about anything else. It says that grass grows in the deepest sea, and it grows above timberline. Grass grows in the highest places and the lowest places on Earth for one reason: grass is obedient to God. It never complains because people walk on it. It never complains because it isn't a tree or that it doesn't have a smell. Grass is just obedient. It just grows where God puts it, so it grows everywhere.

Brother John added that if we could learn this art of surrendering, like the grass, to God, to be just whatever God made you for, just be that person that would be the greatest thing in the world. God wrote the drama of life, and he's never miscast a character. We just sometimes don't want to play the part he gave us because we think that isn't as great a part as someone else might have. However, we should recall what Jesus said, "That he who would be the greatest would be the servant of all."

Estelle Carver told me an interesting fact recently that to me was a revelation. She said the phrase "sincerely yours," which we often use at the end of a letter means more than we may realize. The word "sincere" is from the Latin phrase, "without wax." She said that in ancient Rome, the potter who made a vessel that wasn't just right often took some wax to cover the flaws. He would then paint over the wax and the vessel would "look" perfect. However, when the new owner left the pot in the sun, it would melt and it would become clear that it was an inferior product. The phrase "sincerely yours," affirms that the letter you are writing does not have any wax in it and thus is the real thing and is true.

Our life of love has to be sincere as well. You don't have to be much if you're sincere. You don't need much vanilla extract if it's the real thing. Wood that's pure grain doesn't need varnish. We only varnish wood that is inferior. The church must be sincerely the real thing for Jesus' sake. People have got to experience church members as the real thing and consistently experience them as sincere. Here is a cute story about this subject. I remember that my minister was talking to a parishioner and the man got very angry and said that all of the church members had rubbed him the wrong way. The minister said, "No. You are just turned the wrong way when we're rubbing. We're really trying to pet you."

I have learned that the self that is "crossed" denies the Lord. Every time that anybody has crossed me, I deny the Lord. However, if I am the crossed self – the one with the cross of Jesus on it, that self glorifies God. When I relate to others, I can exhibit the self crossed or the crossed self. In every one of my relationships, I react either one way or the other. I hate to say that most of the time it's the "self-crossed." While some people may never listen to what you say; they do pay deep attention to how you relate to them. Sometimes in our ignorance we walk all over others. We may not mean to do it, but because we are not crossed by Jesus we are not compassionate, we're not tender, and we're not thoughtful. We just don't give ourselves. We withhold ourselves and when that happens, love can't flow.

144

I saw a beautiful wedding ceremony, which I want to tell you about. Let me paint a verbal picture for you. Above the altar was a large cross. And on the altar was a large white candle, unlit. Below the altar on another table were two baskets of flowers and in the middle of each flower basket was a red candle, which had been lit by the church usher.

The bride and groom were married and when the minister pronounced them man and wife, they did not kiss each other. They did something so symbolically beautiful that I was deeply touched. The bride walked over to her flower basket, and the groom walked over to his. Each removed the burning red candle. Together they walked up, lit the white candle, and blew out their candles. Symbolic of what had really happened, each one had surrendered their own light to produce that one light. The two had become one. I'd never seen anything like that before in my life. Then they kissed each other, and then they felt united and we experienced that unison as well.

> **Sometimes in our ignorance we walk all over others. We may not mean to do it, but because we are not crossed by Jesus we are not compassionate, we're not tender, and we're not thoughtful.**

Someone said that marriage is either holy wedlock or unholy deadlock. Amen? God wants us, in our relationship with him, to have holy wedlock where you and I take our candle, walk up to the altar, light the one candle and have union with him. We need to blow out our candle so that we become that through which he can work. We have to give up our candlelight in order for God to have his open channel through us.

When I was a young Christian, I used to ask all kinds of questions. I would say, "Tell me about God." One night I was sitting on our farm house front porch, and it is such a lovely sight to watch the cattle grazing on the hill, and I began to look at the electric wire that went past the house. Someone had told me that the wire carries 6600 volts of electricity. I said to that light wire, "Do you know anything about the kingdom of God that I don't know." Of course, I didn't think it did, but it did. As I was sitting there thinking how many years that light wire had carried 6600 volts of electricity... (It must have been seventy-five years at least) and so I wondered why the light wire didn't wear out. Then I realized the reason. The light wire wasn't doing anything. The electricity was doing the work. The wire was just the conductor of electricity. The wire was open at both ends, one end received the current and the other one distributed it. I felt that if I had the ability of an electric wire, I could be a tremendous Christian. I could be open at both ends and just let God flow through me. I would only have to stay connected. The same goes for the Church. The church just needs to stay connected to the power of Jesus and stay open so His power can run through our church community.

In our spiritual life, I think God wants us to come to a place spiritually where we love Him for nothing. I don't want his gifts. I want Him, the giver of the gifts. I don't want his healing. I want the healer. I don't want the kingdom. I want the king. If I get the king, I'm going to get the kingdom and everything else he's got if I get him. I think sometimes we want God for a reason instead of wanting God for nothing.

This morning I want to tell you a story about what is happening in our church. Our minister is such a wise pastor. For example, when he counsels couples about to be married he offers such unique counseling. He asks the bride to be to sit in one section of the room and the groom in another. He says to the groom, "Here's ten cards all with the number one on it. I want you to tell me why you love this woman. Why do you want to surrender your freedom, go into captivity, and spend all the rest of your life with this one particular woman? What in the world do you see in her that makes you want to do that?" The little bride, is just hoping he gives the right answer. He had better.

The groom sits there and he says the one thing he knows that every woman would love to hear, "She's so beautiful."

The minister says to him, "Well how many points would you give for her beauty?" "Five, man she's beautiful."

The bride's so proud. You know, she's just so pretty. Every woman wants to feel like her husband thinks she is just beautiful. Then the minister says to him, "What else do you like about this girl?"

"Well, she's a brain."

"Well, how many points for a brain?"

"Well, two points for a brain."

Then, "What other thing do you like?"

"Well, she waits on me hand and foot. She makes me feel so comfortable."

"All right. How much for her duty?"

"Well, one point for that."

"All right. Now you've used up eight points," He said, "What else do you love about her. What other thing makes you love this woman and makes you want to spend the rest of you life with her?"

"Well, she's very talented."

"All right, how many points for her talent?"

"One for her talent."

"All right, what else do you like about her?"

"Well she's ... I don't know. She just gives me something. I don't know what. Let's call it ... She's healthy, wealthy, and wise."

"All right, how much for that?"

"One point."

The minister turns to this young man and he said, "I will not marry the two of you. You do not love this woman. You yourself have proven it. If five points of your whole married life is dependent upon the way she looks, son, you don't love her. What if she had an accident and was horribly scarred. Are you going to divorce her and marry a beautiful woman? Do you think this woman's going to have any security knowing that if she gets a wrinkle on her face, your love's going to start to go? Son, love isn't made that way. All right, you said that she waits on you hand and foot. What if she became disabled, and couldn't wait on you hand and foot? Would you be willing to wait on her? Would you put her in a home some place, and marry somebody who could still wait on you. If you want that get a housekeeper, not a wife. All the things that

148

you've said are things that she's going to give you. If that's the only thing you love about her, then you don't love her. Are you going to marry her for herself? You have not included that on your list. Another way to answer this question is to affirm that I am not marrying you for your beauty or your brains, or your talent or for your willingness to take care of me. I am not marrying you for your wealth, or your service to me, but I am only marrying you because of you. I love you for who you are.

That's what God wants the church to do, just love him for nothing. Don't come to church on Sunday morning expecting to get something, but to give something. If nothing else, give the minister

> In our spiritual life, I think God wants us to come to a place spiritually where we love Him for nothing.

a break. Smile at him. Look hungry and thirsty for the word of God and the pastor will preach to quench your thirst. Come to church and start praying for everybody else who came to church hoping that something will happen to them in church. Something will happen in your church because you are bringing in a heart full of the love of God and you don't want anything from the service.

I remember one Sunday I went to church with a very immature outlook. I said to myself and to the Lord, "That Pastor doesn't do anything for me." God said, "Well, what are you doing for him?" I agreed that I was doing nothing for the Pastor and yet I expected something from him. That was not fair. If you have a minister that you don't click with, that is your fault. Find out what makes him tick. Find out what makes him click, what makes him sick. Find out where he's hurting, and love him. Believe in him. Pray for him, and you'll change him because you'll change your attitude about him. When your attitude changes, he will become a different person.

This is what love is all about. Love is a possibility in all of our relationships. Every time I hurt a person, I hurt Jesus. I don't have to be rude or self-centered. I can be a channel of love through which God can work, but sometimes I am not such a channel. That's why I come to Ashrams, and that's why I ask you to pray for me. I want to be a channel of love.

I was speaking recently about the different ways that we can witness to others. I'll tell you one way that will illustrate that you are really a Christian. It's in your willingness and my willingness to admit that we're wrong. I think that's truly a Christian virtue. When you have done something wrong, and God gives you the grace to go and say to that person, "I'm sorry. I'm sorry, and I'm wrong." Not just sorry, a lot of people are sorry because they got caught but they're not sorry they did it. They're sorry it didn't work out that way, but they're not sorry that they did it. I was coming from the Canadian Ashram last year to the Pennsylvania Ashram. It was during the airline strike, and it was at the time when there was both the Fourth of July and the Canadian Dominion Day holidays and so it was a very busy time at the airport.

I had made my reservation to fly from Toronto to Buffalo and then to fly on to Pittsburgh where I was going to be picked up and taken to the Pennsylvania Ashram. I was in great spirits as I started the trip as I had just come from the Toronto Ashram Overflowing Heart experience and everything was going just great. I loved the Lord and loved everybody. See, that was because nobody was crossing me. Everything was going my way, so why wouldn't I be radiant and happy. I'm always radiant and happy when I'm getting everything I want. It's just these other times that are kind of troublesome.

I walked up to the airline ticket counter and since I arrived two hours ahead of time, I expected to be patted on the head for arriving early. I put my ticket down on the counter and said good morning to the agent noting that I had arrived ahead of time. Well, I didn't realize that I wasn't the only customer he'd had that day. It was noon. The strike and the two holidays had probably stressed him out. There were very few airlines that were operating. He asked me my name and I told him as he looked up my reservation in the system and reported that I did not have a reservation. Then this back and forth emerged.

I said, "Sir, there must be some mistake. I have a reservation. I made it myself. It was confirmed a week ago."

He said, "Are you calling me a liar?"

I said, "No. I'm not calling you a liar, but I think you ought to check it out again."

He said, "I don't have to check it out again. You don't have a reservation."

Now you see, I forgot all about Jesus, the Ashram, the wonderful Overflowing Heart. All I could see is here's a guy who's starting something with me and I'm going to finish it. I put down all my religious garments, and I rolled up my sleeves. I said to that guy, "Are you calling me a liar? I made the reservation. I'm a public speaker."

He said, "I don't care who you are, lady. You're not going on this plane!"

I said, "Now sir, I'm going on that plane with or without your help." By that time he dismissed me and took the next customer. The idea! I reached over and picked up my ticket.

He says, "Where are you going with that ticket?"

I said, "It's my ticket isn't it?" I walked around and went to the customs officer.

He says, "Lady, don't get me involved in this. I just check the baggage. I don't have anything to do with the reservations."

I knew I had that reservation. I talked to the head people. I knew I had it. You see, I forgot about Jesus. Here I'm supposed to be witnessing. What's my purpose to get to this Ashram? To tell them about the love of God, and how tender and sweet Jesus is. Here I am clawing this guy to death trying to get to the Christian Ashram.

The agent is supposed to be nice to me. He is hired to be nice to me. I ask him. I said, "Sir, what is your name?"

He said, "My name is John Day."

I said, "I'll make good use of that name sir." I intended to write the airline and tell them what kind of person John Day was. I wasn't going to tell them what kind of person I was. I was going to talk about John Day. By that time another agent came over and said, "Ma'am I'll try to help you, but please don't be so excited." That was the last thing that I wanted to hear. My conscience was saying the same thing and I didn't like that either.

She said to me, "I think I can get you on this plane."

I said, "Don't act like you're doing me a favor, lady. I got a reservation on that flight." She walked down the ramp with me, and made me carry both of my heavy bags. I packed them, but I didn't want to carry them. I expected a porter to do that for me, so I didn't care how heavy they were. They didn't charge you for weight in those days. She made me carry them down the steps. When you're not in the Lord, oh things are heavy! I was so mad, you know. I was just thinking about how they're treating me. I'll never come back to Canada. They'd already asked me to come back to the Canadian Ashram, and I'd already made up my mind. No! I'm not going back because I was mad.

I got to the airplane. The attendant says to me, "Why in the world are you carrying your own bags?"

I said, "That's a good question sir." I handed them to him and told him that I was carrying them because they wouldn't send them down on the conveyor belt. I wasn't going to act nice if they weren't going to act nice. Well that sure makes for good, doesn't it?

I got in the airplane. The stewardess said to me, "Would you like a newspaper?" It was a Canadian paper. I wouldn't read a Canadian paper for anything. I said, "No, thank you."

The flight to Buffalo was just ten minutes and the pilot said we are now flying over the Canadian Falls. "All of you on the left side, look out the window."

Love is a possibility in all of our relationships. Every time I hurt a person, I hurt Jesus... I can be a channel of love through which God can work...

I thought, "I wouldn't look at the Canadian Falls, I would wait until I could see the American Falls." I was crying, I was mad, I was hurt and I was worried. I thought, "Now when I get to Buffalo and if don't have the reservation on to Pittsburgh, what am I going to do? I don't have enough money to stay in a hotel. What if I can't get to the Ashram, I am already one day late. If I get there two days late, I won't even get paid. I won't even be useful at all." Among all of these frustrations, I did not once think about Jesus.

When we arrived in Buffalo, I went over to the American Airlines ticket counter and said, "Sir, are you holding a confirmed reservation for Mrs. Webster on your flight?"

He said, "Yes ma'am, we are."

I said, "Did I have a flight reservation on the Mohawk?"

"Yes, you did."

"Confirmed?"

"Yes."

Okay, now I was right. The trouble is you can't be right and be a Christian. You've got to give up your being right. As I turned to call Mr. Day, and tell him what I thought of him, I ran into Jesus.

Now, this is an amazing thing. I wouldn't believe it if it hadn't happened to me. When the phone was answered the man said, "This is John Day speaking."

I said, "John Day, this is Mrs. Webster. I'm in Buffalo and I did have a confirmed flight on Mohawk Airlines. I didn't call you up to tell you that. I called you to tell you how terribly sorry I am for being the kind of person I am and the kind of person I was toward you. I'm supposed to

154

be a Christian, but God knows I'm so far from it that it isn't even funny. The least little thing, and I blow up. I'm sorry I offended you and took out my upset and all my problems out on you, because I know that I am not the only customer you have.

A miracle happened. The man said, "Mrs. Webster, you were right all along and I knew it. Boy, I've had it. I've had it till today, and I was right up to here!" He said, "Everything I've done today is wrong, and I couldn't be wrong one more time. I'm a man, and I've got to have some self-respect. I didn't want that woman at the ticket counter rubbing it in to me, so I didn't care whether you liked it or not. I couldn't help it. I just reacted. He said, "I am sorry. That's not way to act, but at that time I didn't care."

We meet a lot of people like that. That's why Jesus expects us to be different, not the same as them, not to treat them like they may be treating us. I had forgotten about that wonderful opportunity that I had to witness. I goofed. All I did was react. I said, "Well John Day, I didn't call you up to get an apology from you, but to ask you to forgive me. I'm terribly sorry that I am this way."

You know, he said, "I'm terribly sorry I'm this way."

I said, "Well, I'm asking God to forgive me. I'm asking you to forgive me."

He said, "Well, I'll forgive you if you'll forgive me." He said, "Please come back to Canada again, and don't blame Mohawk Airlines for what I did."

I said, "Well, don't blame America for what I did." Here we end up loving each other. I could have done that in the first place, but not me. I got to go the old hard way around. As someone said, "The way of the transgressor is hard." If you are going to act that way and react that way, you don't glorify God.

I then got on the airplane and flew to Pittsburgh. I was thanking God that Brother Stanley was there to take the night meeting because then I'd have all night to recuperate from my upset. See, I couldn't get up and talk when I'm all shook up, especially about victory when you don't have any.

When I got there the brother who picked me up was so glad to see me. He said, "Brother Stanley isn't able to be here. We need you to speak the minute you arrive. And now there was a long car trip ahead of me and I'm supposed to speak right away. I thought, "Oh no, Lord. No! No! No! I can't." Then I said to the brother, "Well, it's a good thing that I got here. I almost didn't get here." Then I thought, "What did I say that for? Now I've got to explain." The first thing I knew, I had to tell him the whole story.

When I got to the Ashram, I kept saying, "Oh Holy Spirit, give me something to say. Give me something to say. Give me something to say." When I stood up, he gave me something to say. He made me tell the whole story about Mr. Day and Mohawk Airlines. I did and this little boy came up to me afterwards.

He said, "I'm from Formosa (Taiwan). If you'd have said anything else tonight except what you did say, I wouldn't have bought it." He said to me, "How many children do you have?"

I said, "I have two sons."

He said, "May I be your number three son?" He's got his name in my Bible, number three son.

You see, Jesus can use you if you'll let him, if you are willing. I didn't want to act that way. I have asked God to help me not act that way.

A lovely thing happened to me last Christmas. I was fixing dinner for all of us. We always do that at Christmas. However at Christmas we are often not thinking of anybody but ourselves. We buy presents and give them to our loved ones. We eat the food we want. We haven't even got time to go to church. We're just busy, busy, busy, busy, busy. We don't read the Bible. We don't pray. We could never have a revival at Christmas time. "Are you out of your mind," they would say, "It's Christmas! We've got to do something else. You haven't even got your presents bought. You haven't sent your cards out. Are you crazy to think about having a revival at Christmastime?"

Our families now share our Christmas presents for each other about three days before Christmas, so that on Christmas day we can give the whole day over to God to think about his son and what he did for us. We don't want to be all involved with our own selves, what we're doing, and what we want. I had the Christmas Eve dinner almost ready and after we ate it, we were going to church together. When you have a lot of people and you're getting a big dinner, the best thing people can do is just stay out of the kitchen. However, ten minutes before six, and we were about to eat at six to be at church at seven, my oldest boy Ted wanted to make ice cream. He had given my sister-in-law something he always wanted for Christmas, an electric ice cream maker. He said to his brother, "Come on! Let's make some homemade ice cream!" He had no idea what it takes to make ice cream.

I said, "Son, we haven't got time to make it now. It's time to go to church."

He said, "I know, but we can make it and we won't bother you."

The stove's full of stuff. You can't have boys in the kitchen who don't know how to cook making ice cream. It takes half an hour to make the custard and then you have to let it cool. You then have to freeze it and then do all sorts of other things. I saw there was no point in telling Ted all of that. He had his heart set on making ice cream.

I said, "Son, we haven't got time. Let's just let it go."

He said, "You never want me to do anything I want to do, do you?"

I recall a time when I would just have burst into tears. Our whole Christmas would have been ruined. I didn't even answer him. By the power of God, I just didn't even answer him. That's a miracle. Then his brother came in and said something. I just went ahead and got the supper on the table, and after we ate it, we went to church.

After we came home, I said, "Come on. Let's make our ice cream."

"Nope. You didn't want to make it when we wanted. We don't have to make it when you want to."

I said, "Okay. I'll make it all by myself. Maybe you'll feel like eating it."

Pretty soon they came into the kitchen. Teddy said to me, "Mother, I didn't know it took so long to make ice cream. I just thought it would be just like that."

I said, "I know you didn't know honey. That's what a mother is for. She knows, and she sometimes she doesn't. She just goes ahead and does what she knows is right, no matter how much you complain."

He said, "Mother, I'm awfully sorry that I said that to you. I really didn't mean it."

Isn't it wonderful that God gives you the power to say, "I'm sorry. I'm wrong." He does when we're really sorry. Our greatest witness comes when we're willing to go back and apologize. Others know then that God's working in our life.

I fell in love with the Holy Spirit at Christmas last year. Really fell in love with him, just like I did when I met Jesus. You go with a person for a long time before you really fall in love with them. When you love them, you just love them because you don't know why you love them. You just do. I had the strangest experience.

I went to the minister and I said, "I don't know what in the world is the matter with me. I get in my car, I start to drive, and I begin to think about God. I end up ... I don't even know where I am, or what in the world I'm doing, or where I'm going. I've got to go back to where I started to find out where I'm supposed to be going. What's happening to me? I'm just getting lost in the Lord. I got to stay on this Earth. There's things I have to do, and I can't be running back and forth forgetting where I should be going.

I fell in love with the Holy Spirit at Christmas last year. Really fell in love with him, just like I did when I met Jesus. You go with a person for a long time before you really fall in love with them.

I began to love the Lord for nothing. I walked into our church one Sunday morning, and I had never realized before what it meant in Haggai (2:6-7) when the writer said, "Once again, in a little while I will shake the heavens and the earth and the sea and the dry land; and I will shake all nations, so that the treasures of all nations shall come in, and I will fill this house with splendor, says the lord of hosts. " I walked into my own church on Sunday morning with that verse in my heart.

Now our church is like every normal church. I've been in that church when you could cut the hate that was there between the members with a knife. You could feel it. We were functioning under the sham of religion but you could feel the hate. This particular Sunday morning when I went to church, I felt like it was Thanksgiving Day, you know. Everybody's happy, and everybody's thankful. I just loved everybody in that church. I knew the secrets of most of those people. I knew where they had come from and how God had begun to work in their lives, the troubles that they were dealing with and I could just feel that I loved them.

We were at the place in the service where we say the Lord's Prayer. As soon as it was over, I don't know what in the world came over me but all of a sudden, I just said right out loud. I said, "Forest, Would you sing for us? Everybody loves to hear you sing in this church." He's got a beautiful voice. He's a Welshman, and the Welsh have this kind of marvelous quality in their voice. I don't know what it is. It just does something to you. I said, "Would you sing the Old Rugged Cross?"

It just completely floored him. He's never had anybody break up his service like this. He went over and he got the hymnal. He didn't look at us. He just looked at the words. All of us were looking beyond the minister to the picture of Jesus on the wall. Forrest sang through tears. He just cried the song. At the end, we were all broken up. Everybody in that room was crying. I don't know why they were crying. The Lord had come. He was there, and everybody could feel his presence.

I sniffled and sniffled like everybody else, you know. I was embarrassed. I thought, "I got to stop this," but everybody was so moved. Then Forrest offered the Pastoral Prayer but when he got just three sentences into the Pastoral Prayer, the Spirit hit us again. Everybody started crying again. It was just like God took that little old white church sitting out there in the country with 200 old farmers in it, and he just took it and just shook it just like Haggai said. Just like he's going to shake the devil out of it. Isn't that wonderful? The Lord just shook it!

I was crying so hard, I just didn't know what to do. I thought, "I've just got to get out of this building, out of this place or I am going to explode with the love of God, it's just too much." I thought I would never "survive" until the pastor gained control of himself and went on with the service. You know, something happened that Sunday. When we went out, one of the least spiritual people (although I have to admit that we really never know how spiritual people are) spoke to the pastor. Anyway, this little woman went out and said to the preacher, "Forrest, when you were singing The Old Rugged Cross, if you had given an altar call, we'd have mobbed each other getting to the altar."

He said, "I didn't have to give an altar call. We were all already there."

Were you there when they crucified the Lord? I think every person there saw themselves at the crucifixion that Sunday morning. We weren't looking at others. We were looking at Jesus. When you look at Jesus and really see him, you see yourself. You don't see the other person's faults. You love the other person. That other person is sort of a comfort to you because he's got some faults that you can identify with.

Something else quite wonderful happened in our little church that Sunday morning. God gave me a whole new conception of the Ten Commandments. You know when you look at them through the perspective of law, they look like laws. Thou shalt not do this. Thou shalt not do that. Thou shalt not steal. Thou shalt not covet. On that Sunday morning, I knew what the Ten Commandments were. They're just God's promises. When you love me enough you won't commit adultery, you won't have other Gods before me, you won't lie, you won't cheat, you won't steal. You couldn't. You're going to have so much love, you're just going to love people. That's all God wants the church to do, not to see those commandments as things you can't do. You would not even want to do such things, when love hits you!

God made marriage so that we could know on Earth what heaven is like. You've got a father, you got a mother, and you've got a child because you've got a father, a son, and a holy spirit. I remember one morning, I was asking the Lord. I said, "I don't understand this trinity. What is a trinity? "

I was listening to the radio downstairs that one son had playing and the other son was upstairs listening to the identical program on his radio. When I was downstairs,

I could hear the downstairs radio predominantly, but the upstairs radio only faintly. Then I went upstairs, and I could hear the upstairs radio predominantly, and the downstairs radio only faintly. When I stood on the stairs half way between the two radios, you know it was stereo. I couldn't tell where they started and stopped. They were all flowing together.

I knew then what the trinity was. Sometimes, the father is working on me. Sometimes, the son is working on me. Sometimes, the holy spirit is working on me. Sometimes, they're all working on me. God, who is present in the every day things of our life, begins to show forth his glory. All he asks us to do is to take off our shoes and sit down and listen to him. He's broadcasting twenty-four hours a day.

I hope when you go home from this Ashram, you will just tell people how you feel about God. Just get up say something. Well I don't mean give a speech. However, if a man in your office is swearing, don't pull away from him. Go over to him, and talk to him. Put your arm around him and say, "Buddy, I know how you feel." You can identify with him. That's witnessing. For example, you can say, "I sometimes feel the same way. I'd do the

God gave me a whole new conception of the Ten Command- ments. You know when you look at them through the perspective of law, they look like laws. Thou shalt not do this... On that Sunday morning, I knew what the Ten Commandments were. They're just God's promises.

163

same thing if I didn't know Jesus. He's really helped me to keep from getting stomach ulcers. When I used to get all mad, and all upset I would get sick. I got tired of getting sick, so I got saved. Now, I'm not feeling that way anymore. If you had this Jesus in your life, you wouldn't either." That man will want to know what happened in your life.

If you see somebody who is lying in the gutter. Don't stand over him and say, "I just don't see how you ever got there." God doesn't ask you to just stare. He says get the man out. Get down on your knees and say, "The only difference between you and me is that I got out of the gutter, and you're still there. God can help you out with the same ladder he helped me. He brought me Jesus into my life."

God doesn't ask us to do anything that's impossible to do. You know people that I don't know, and I know people that you don't know. Whenever you feel the urge to say or to go and get some other Christian to do what God's laying on your heart, don't. Just go and do what God's laying on your heart. If you know somebody who isn't saved just talk to her. You know the plan of salvation. You know the Lord Jesus, and God wants you to start witnessing. We pray for a thousand tongues, but we don't even use the one we have got. I believe that God is going to come into this moment and help us learn to love each other for nothing. Love your wife that way. You know, if any man loved his wife that way, she's just bound to love him back that way.

Life begets life. If a wife loved her husband as unto the Lord, she's just bound to get the same love back. We had a woman at the Ashram who told me that she didn't love her husband, that she's going to get a divorce. She's been married to him for twelve years, and they fought every minute of those years. Unholy deadlock, I said, "You're lying to me aren't you. You're kidding yourself. If you wanted to get a divorce, you would be talking to a lawyer, not to Christian who doesn't believe in divorce. You want me to talk you out of it. You love the guy, but your pride's involved."

Then her pride really got involved. She said, "Well, how dare you talk to me this way."

I said, "Honey, I wouldn't even be talking to you this way if you hadn't come to me. You want me to help you, or hurt you, or what?"

I said to her, "But it is your pride. Would you rather have your way and lose your husband, or to give up your way, find your husband, and have a married life? You love the guy, but you don't know how to get along with him, communicate, and relate to him."

She said, "Now, just what would you suggest that I do?"

I knew she wasn't going to like it. I said, "Well, go home and tell your husband that it's your fault that you don't get along."

She said, "Well, that's just what he says. I'm not going home and agree with him."

I said, "Okay. You don't need a change of husband. You need a change of heart. If you had a change of heart, that husband that you have would be wonderful." I said, " You're going to make a big mistake. You can get another husband, but you're still going to be you unless Jesus changes that attitude in you. You're hard honey. Why is

165

it so hard for you to let your husband have what he wants? Because you want what you want, I know."

That woman, it took a lot of Jesus to get her to bend the knee and say to God, "Help me Lord. I'm supposed to be a Christian, but I don't act like it. I'm expecting my husband who says he isn't a Christian to act like a Christian for my sake."

Do you know, I told her to read everyday the story of the crucifixion until she knew it was her "fault" that Jesus died. You know, she wrote me a letter afterwards. I still have the letter. She said that she went home and she did what I suggested. She got her husband's breakfast, and the shock nearly killed him.

She said when he came downstairs, he was so surprised because she hadn't been doing that for years. She said she was cooking his breakfast at the stove when he came in. He sat down at the table, and he didn't know what to say. Finally, she said he pulled his napkin across his lap in that conceited way and said, "Well, Miss High and Mighty, what did you get out of this retreat?"

That's a lovely opportunity to witness. She said, "I was standing at the stove with this skillet in my hand, which I thought about throwing at him but I had the strangest experience. The story of the crucifixion saved me. I knew that Jesus died because I felt like throwing that skillet. Not that I did it, but that I even felt like doing it." She said in that moment, "I said, 'I'm sorry, Lord.'" She said, "Jesus gave me the power to go and kneel before my husband, and say, 'I learned this week that I'm the reason we don't get along. It's my fault and I'm sorry. I found the Lord. I found forgiveness. I want to live with you for six weeks this way, and love you for nothing. If that doesn't work and you want a divorce, I'll let you have it.'"

She continued, "I didn't know what to do. I waited for him to say something or to agree with me, and say he was glad that I found that I was the reason. However, he almost knocked the dishes off the table he got on his knees so fast and took me in his arms, right there on our kitchen floor."

He said, "Darling, for twelve years I've been trying to tell you I'm sorry, but you won't let me say I'm sorry. You would just react negatively to everything I do. I am sorry! I don't want to hurt you. I love you, but I don't know how to tell you I love you." He added, "Really, it's not your fault alone. It's just as much my fault as yours. In fact, it's more my fault that yours."

> **You know the plan of salvation. You know the Lord Jesus, and God wants you to start witnessing.**

She said, "We almost got into an argument over whose fault it was. Now we both wanted to take the blame." She said, "There after twelve years of being tied together by a legal knot, we were really married by God and became one. We had only one will between us, God's will." She said, "We became leaders in a Fisherman's Club in our community. We decided that we would go out and give this gift of God to every unhappy couple that we knew. We would talk to the man about his life with God, and the woman with her life with God, and then bring them together and see what would happen."

She said, "Every time a man and his wife come together and experience this gift, we ask them to go out and find another person and give it away again." She said, "We have six couples already helping others. Praise the Lord." See, that's the church at work. We are going home in the name and the power of Jesus Christ, and letting him work through us. Now it may not work perfectly every time, but the wonderful thing is that you can fall on your knees, tell him you're sorry, and get up and keep on going.

Let us pray:

Father, we just love everybody in this room because you love us. You give us the power to love each other. You give us tears to cry, and you give us arms to love, and hands to serve, and feet to do things for people. Help us to make use of these wonderful abilities to show you how much we love you by doing everything we do in your name and in your spirit to somebody else. Help us in our relationships with our friends, to remember the story of the rose. Not to cut the rose and keep it for ourselves, but to leave it alone. Let it grow where everybody can see it. Help us, Father, to witness and become the church at work about our Father's business. We ask it in Jesus' name, Amen.

Mary Webster: Jesus is Lord!

Mary Webster, E. Stanley Jones and others, 1967: The editor was with Mary in India during this time.

FOUR

WHAT HAPPENS WHEN
WE TAKE OUR EYES
OFF JESUS?

INTRODUCTION

Mary is bold and forthright in exposing her occasional spiritual and emotional immaturities in this talk. Her frank sharing of her own shortcomings is a gentle invitation for us to reflect on our own. The reader is surely tempted to do so and Mary points the way to move toward spiritual and emotional maturity.

This morning, I would like to share with you something that is very important to me and I hope that in sharing my story, that I will be able to save you some heartache. In our early lives as Jesus followers, we are sometimes discouraged and say to ourselves, "What is the use? I can't do all these "good" things. I can't really be a Christian." I want to say that as long as you keep your eyes on Jesus, all will be well. However, I am going to tell you a few stories about what happened to me, when I did not keep my eyes on Jesus. I hope that my cautionary tales will be of help to each of you.

Before Mary is able to surrender and simply let the Lord "work on her" she experiences considerable distress as she fails to communicate with another culture. Her provincialism is stunning and her inability to think before she speaks may remind us of our "occasional" selves.

I had been given the opportunity to travel to Korea and Japan with Brother Stanley and Brother Tom for three months and it sounded just terrific. I figured that because the Lord saw that I had enough on the ball He was going to send me to those far away countries to tell them the Good News. I was quick to find out that that was not why the Lord sent me.

Now I thought I was a pretty mature Christian and you can feel that way as well for a while until the Lord sees what you really need and starts working on you. When you're in a perfect situation and everything's going the way you want it, that is easy and so it is possible to believe that you are mature. You feel mature, but that is not always the case and I learned this from experience.

For a long time, I felt secure in the Lord and I felt happy and believed that I was balanced. I didn't get real high and I didn't get real low and I was having a terrific time. However, my "balanced" experience was illusory and separated me from others who were going up and down like an elevator and who sometimes felt "out of control." The Lord had to take me down a notch or two so He let me go "up and down" and feel out of control just so I'd know that I was similar to others on their Christian journey, and that I was not particularly special.

Mary learned very quickly and painfully that she was sharing the gospel with her mouth but not living it with her life. Mary was taking her eyes off Jesus.

When life is fine and I get my own way, I'm a tremendous Christian, but, boy, when things don't go my way, I go down like a house of cards and I had to learn that. I had to see that weakness in me in order to face it and get victory over it.

Read on to discover how in spite of Mary's initial reactions the Lord offered her a path to victory as she learns the definition of grace...and of course the critical importance of keeping her eyes on Jesus.

THIS MORNING, I WOULD like to share with you something that is very important to me and I hope that in sharing my story, that I will be able to save you some heartache. In our early lives as Jesus followers, we are sometimes discouraged and say to ourselves, "What is the use? I can't do all these "good" things. I can't really be a Christian." However, I want to say that as long as you keep your eyes on Jesus, all will be well. However, I am going to tell you a few stories about what happened to me, when I did not keep my eyes on Jesus. I hope that my cautionary tales will be of help to each of you.

At an Ashram, there are so many of us at all different stages of our Christian Life. For example, Brother Stanley has been a Christian for more than 50 years and so he can look back and describe his experiences as he has had lots of practice being a Christian. For me, when I look at a Christian who is farther up the road than I am, it can become discouraging. If you listen to somebody talk about too much victory and you're in defeat, it can have a demoralizing effect.

I want to share with you this morning something about "Victory" that I think is important. Where do you get the victory that all these other Christians are talking about? I think it's sometimes more helpful in an Ashram to share the defeats that you've had than to share the victories. And sometimes when we only share victories, we separate ourselves from others and lose the sense that we are all on this Christian journey together! There isn't anybody sitting here that doesn't have something in their life that the Lord Jesus is working on.

I've never met a perfect person yet. I remember a real spiritual struggle I had a few years ago. I almost lost my faith in the Lord. I almost lost everything because I put my eyes on a Christian, instead of on Christ, and I went down for the count. It doesn't take much to get your eyes off of Jesus. It doesn't matter what you're looking at. If you're looking at yourself, if you're looking at your neighbor, if you're looking at some bad situation, it doesn't matter what it is, if you take your eyes off of Jesus, you fall. That is what happens.

This morning, I'd like to speak about spiritual and emotional immaturity and how to go from immaturity to spiritual and emotional healing. What happens? Where is the victory coming from? I think if we can understand this, we would be less stressed and move along joyfully on our Christian journey.

Now I thought I was a pretty mature Christian and you can feel that way as well for a while until the Lord sees what you really need and starts working on you. When you're in a perfect situation and everything's going the way you want it, it is easy and so it is easy to believe that you are mature. You feel mature, but that is not always the case and I know this from experience.

For a long time, I felt secure in the Lord and I felt happy and balanced. I didn't get real high and I didn't get real low and I was having a terrific time. However, my "balanced" experience separated me from others who were going up and down like an elevator and sometimes they felt "out of control." The Lord had to take me down a notch or two so He let me go "up and down" and feel out of control quite a few times just so I'd know that I was similar to others on the Christian journey, and not particularly special.

God took me from what I felt was a well-deserved very perfect situation where everything was just right and put me in a place where everything was quite wrong. I wasn't in that new situation for five minutes before I knew how spiritually and emotionally immature I really was. I had to experience it! Now if the Lord had sent some nice Christian into my life, who would tell me how spiritually insecure and emotionally immature I was, I would not have listened to her. I would have defended myself and rejected her comments, but Jesus doesn't give advice, he provides experience. Jesus provided me an experience where I could see for myself what was wrong and as soon as I saw it, nobody had to tell me I was emotionally and spiritually immature. I sure saw it and as soon as I experienced that revelation, I was back in God's hands and I could grow and change.

I had been given the opportunity to travel to Korea and Japan with Brother Stanley and Brother Tom for three months and it sounded just terrific. I figured that the Lord saw that I had enough on the ball that He was going to send me to those far away countries so I could share the Good News. I was quick to find out that that was not why the Lord sent me to Asia.

Rather the Lord wanted me to realize through some very painful experiences that I was not as great a Christian as I thought I was and that I just didn't have what I thought I had. It was not long after our arrival in Japan when I knew something was very wrong. The first thing I did, after leaving that airport was to tell the cab driver "You drive down the wrong side of the street." He said, "Oh, no, we don't. We drive down the left side of the street." Who did I think I was to open my big mouth and make that comment? I thought that if people don't drive down the side of the street that I am used to, that they are wrong, not me. They were driving down the left side of the street, not the wrong side."

My unfortunate behavior and comments continued. We visited a Buddhist temple that held hundreds of urns full of the ashes of dead people. Outside of the temple was food in little bowls and so I said to the guide, "Do they really think that these dead ashes are going to come out and eat this food?"

> God took me from what I felt was a well-deserved very perfect situation where everything was just right and put me in a place where everything was just wrong.

"Oh," he responded, "We believe that our ancestors will smell the flowers that are brought to the temple and then be hungry enough to eat the food." Now I didn't intend to insult the Japanese. I didn't mean to act as if I believed that Americans were more sophisticated and the Japanese were less so or primitive and unscientific, but that's the impression that I gave. I was exhibiting my emotional and spiritual immaturity. When you speak without thinking about what you're saying, without thinking of how it's going to be heard and experienced by somebody else, you are emotionally and spiritually immature. Unfortunately people do those things sometimes and I sure did!

I know that I did not mean to be unkind, but I spoke without thinking and then had to go back and apologize for my words. However, the apology never fully takes away the sting. If you tell a person something in a fit of temper and you go back later and say, "I didn't mean it." The recipient of your anger still feels the harsh words, don't they? If you didn't really mean it, you should not have said it. You must have meant it at least a bit. You couldn't have said it if you didn't and so I began to see that every time I opened my mouth, I put my foot in it and ended up having something to apologize for.

God had to make me feel this way because I was just too cocky for my own good. I thought that I just couldn't do anything wrong. I was too secure and too wrapped up in myself and forgot about others and spoke without thinking. I was immature.

Jesus helped me come to grips with my cockiness and illusions about how special I was. I found out rather quickly that I wasn't the kind of a Christian who should go to Japan to preach the Gospel. I had to go to Japan to realize that I really didn't know (or live) the real Gospel. I was talking the Gospel with my mouth but not living it with my life.

It gets worse... I did not pay any attention to the orientation that we received about Japanese culture. I was speaking through an interpreter and I was trying to tell the Japanese people in my own way that they were teaching me important things about my faith but I conveyed my thoughts very inappropriately and

WHAT HAPPENS WHEN WE TAKE...

inelegantly. I compared my ten-room house to their tiny apartments and my power lawn mower to the scissors they used to trim their grass. I was trying to confess that I took so much for granted in my life and the Japanese had so little and that I appreciated them. However, what I intended by my use of words was not at all what my Japanese audience heard. After my little talk, our host missionary came over to me and said, "I have never been so ashamed of anybody in my life. Who do you think you are? You've done more damage in five minutes than the good we've been able to do in 25 years." I replied, "What? What did I do?" He said, "You have no right to come over here and flaunt your wealth in the face of these people." I wasn't trying to do that, but that's what he thought I was doing. Now he should have told me that at the orientation meeting that you never talk about material things to the Japanese. He may well have given that advice but since I was not paying attention, oh my. I was in 'trouble.'

My heart was just crushed and do you want to know what I did first, or what I really did? My first reaction was to keep my eyes on Jesus and I should have followed that impulse and gone to that man and said, "Thank you for telling me something that I really needed to know. I really didn't mean any harm but I've hurt somebody because I'm thoughtless and I'm immature. Pray for me and from this, I'm going on and I'm going to witness in a way that I won't hurt the Japanese people."

However, I didn't go with my first impulse, what I really did was to take my eyes off of Jesus Christ and focused them on that missionary who offended me and so I said to him, "I didn't come across the ocean to insult the Japanese people. I came over here to help them. I love

179

them. I'd give them the shirt off of my back." I was mad because I was really hurt. The missionary made me just feel awful and so I did the perfectly normal thing to do when you take your eyes off of Jesus which is to focus on yourself and self-pity steps in.

I really wanted to run and hide and lick my wounds and feel sorry for myself. That night I didn't go to the meeting, I went up in my bedroom and I just bawled my eyes out and I said, "Jesus, I didn't want to come over to this darn old country anyway. I don't like this place. I don't like the food. I don't like the people. I want to go home." I knew I couldn't go home. Somebody had spent a lot of money to pay my way over there and I knew that I would have to stay.

Moreover, Jesus didn't help me any, because He didn't take my side. He didn't say the missionary was wrong. He said my reaction was wrong to what the missionary said to me and He brought me to Asia because I was emotionally and spiritually immature. I had a painful lesson to learn. I didn't have to act that way because grace was available to me, I just wouldn't accept it. I wasn't looking at Jesus, I was looking at me and Jesus proved his point.

The next day we got on a train and I was hopeful that perhaps things would go better. Once we were on the train, I sat across from Brother Tom. The interpreter and Brother Stanley were in the seats in front of us. Some of the women who had attended my talk the day before came over to tell Brother Stanley about what I had said. They did not notice that I was nearby and could hear them. Brother Stanley was horrified with what they told him.

Again, my first thought was to go to the women and say, "Pray for me, I'm just an ignorant peasant. I don't know anything, pray for me, and thank you." However, I didn't because again, I took my eyes off of Jesus. I looked at the woman, instead of Jesus Christ. I then burst into tears. Brother Tom did not intervene, and he didn't come over and say, "You poor little thing. Those women had no right to talk about you." He just sat there and read a book. I thought, "Why doesn't he minister to me? He's a minister and I'm heartbroken. He's not doing a thing to help me out."

You see, he couldn't and neither could God because I wouldn't accept the grace that was available to me. Once again I was willing to take my eyes off of Jesus and the same thing happened again that had occurred the

When you speak without thinking about what you're saying, without thinking of how it's going to be heard and experienced by somebody else, you are emotionally and spiritually immature.

day before. I hadn't learned a thing from that previous days event and so Jesus again simply showed me how immature I was.

When life is fine and I get my own way, I'm a tremendous Christian, but, boy, when things don't go my way, I go down like a house of cards and I had to learn that. I had to see it in me in order to face it and get victory over it. However at that moment, I was just so wrapped up in self-pity that I wouldn't talk to the interpreter. I

181

thought I had ruined my relationship with him. How can he interpret for me if I had insulted his people?

I felt just terrible and said to Brother Stanley, "You brought me over here and you can make me go to these meetings but you can't make me get up and say anything, because I'm not going to open my mouth again, not as long as I'm in Japan. Everything I have said was wrong, and believe me, nobody else is going to find fault with the way I witness for Jesus because I'm not going to talk about Him again, ever, to anybody, and as soon as I get back to America, I'm going to get a job in a travel agency and forget the whole business."

You know what he did? He said, "Go ahead, but you won't change Jesus." Brother Stanley did not engage in my pity party. He didn't try to sympathize with me or make an effort for me to feel better. It is a good thing that he did not because he would have only made me more delinquent than I was and he was just wise enough to let me stew in my own juice until God showed me what He wanted to show me. You can't help a person get out of a mess until they figure out what the mess is about and their role in contributing to the mess. But, the mess was not over yet...

The next day, when we were discussing my turn to speak at the Ashram, I said to Brother Stanley "You can't make me stand up to speak. I'll just stand up there and embarrass you all. I'll just stand up there and won't say a word. I can't. I have no witness. I'm a horrible person. I'm broken. I've reached the end of my rope."

I went into the prayer room and I prayed for two solid hours. I wished that God would just come and bring His Presence back to me. However, the Presence had never left. I had left the Presence. I'd gone away from Jesus by taking my eyes off of Him, and by not doing what the Spirit wanted me to do. I sure gave the devil a wonderful opportunity to come back again into my life full force and he did!

I couldn't pray. I couldn't even make contact with Jesus and when I came out of the prayer room, I was just so sad. I didn't want to look at anybody. I didn't want anybody to look at me. I wanted to cry and I had cried so much already that I couldn't cry anymore. There weren't any more tears. I was completely broken. Brother Tom came up to me and said, "How are you coming along with your pity party, Mary?"

Brother Tom knew that I was awash with pity and I had to admit that his observation was true. But I felt the "sting" of his words. To me that was a sign that the Lord is really showing me something. Remember the woman at the well, Jesus named her and when she felt the sting, she found healing. You see she had to feel a sting in order to experience a healing. How would she know what healing meant if she didn't experience the sting of brokenness? That had to come first and so I thought, "Well..."

Brother Tom said, "You know, Mary, these people didn't like the way you held the bat yesterday when you got up to hit," and, "If I were you, I'd pick up that bat again and I'd just knock a home run for the Lord right out into center field." I responded, "I'm not going to knock a home run and I'm not going to strike out because I'm not even going up to bat." I said, "I can't. I just can't. You don't understand. You don't know."

183

God then sent the only person to me who could help me. Suddenly my interpreter whom I thought I had deeply offended came over to me when it was it was my time to speak and put his arm around me and said, "Come on, honey. Let's go." I couldn't have done anything but go with him for he was essentially saying, "I love you. I don't care what you've done. I love you. I know you didn't mean any harm. I understand."

I could see through him the heart of God. When we went into the pulpit together, we had the most wonderful connection. I just loved that man and to think that he forgave me. I didn't even ask him to do it. I didn't have grace enough to even ask him to forgive me, but when he translated my words, the feeling of compassion and tenderness was powerful. God was using my message through his words and I believe that he said things that I know I wasn't saying. He made my words sound so good, I've never seen people respond to a message like that but you see the love of God was in him.

No matter what was in me, the grace of God was in him and working through him and people were blessed and so was I! When we left the church, I still felt badly but I knew that I had learned something. The grace of God is the most tremendous thing in the world and many of us don't even realize or appreciate its power and love until you really need it. I really needed it and I really appreciated it.

When we have known the love of Jesus and then have it "vanish" you realize how desperately you need Him in your life. For me I had to learn the hard way what would happen to me if I took my eyes off of Jesus. I never wanted to leave Him again.

I am reminded of an illustration from our farm. We have sheep and the Lord has used sheep to show me important faith and life messages. When I was a young Christian, I would just study sheep and their relationships with each other. I watched what they did and they taught me a lot about the kingdom of God. I watched the ewes, and their little lambs would come up and nurse and noticed that as soon as their stomachs were full, they would go on off like kids do at a picnic and run off by themselves.

The ewes would stay still and just chew their cud real slowly as they weren't going anywhere, but the little lambs would just run and chase each other all around the farm yard. I saw one of the lambs run around the barn. He got out of the sight of his mother. The other little lambs came back to the front of the barn, but the

> **You can't help a person get out of a mess until they figure out what the mess is about and their role in contributing to the mess.**

little lamb did not come with them. He looked around with this, "Where did my momma go? I'm lost," look and he cried. Now I watched his mother. When the first cry came, she stopped chewing and she listened but she didn't move. Then he cried again and this time, she continued to just stand perfectly still and listen. When the baby lamb now cried panic stricken the third time, she went to get him. You know, I watched that little lamb the next night, he did not leave his mother's side at all. The feeling of being away from his mother, that horrible, panicky feeling of being lost, was so awful and so new to him that the next night he did not go and play with the little lambs. He stayed right by his mother where he could feel secure.

Using that illustration, I could see myself running away from Jesus, feeling lost and being left "lost," so the next time, I wouldn't run away. The next time, I'd obey the Holy Spirit and do what He told me to do. I began to see that this is the way God gives you the victory. If you don't have any defeats, you can't have any victories.

Here is another story, and I need to say up front, I just despise the white part of egg. One day at an Ashram, I went down for breakfast and saw that they were serving eggs. I said, "Oh, praise the Lord, we've got eggs for breakfast." My friend said, "You like eggs?" I said, "I hate them." She said, "What are you so happy about then?" I said, "I'm going to get a victory. I'm going to eat eggs for Jesus' sake." She said, "Well, I love eggs." I said, "Yes, but you can't get a victory and I can because I hate them and I'm going to eat them anyway." You see we can't have everything perfect to have victory because victory comes out of the ashes of the old things.

Now another experience about the need for victory – this time my story is back in Japan. I was annoyed that the mail from my family was not getting to me in a timely fashion. I noticed that my fellow travelers, Brother Tom and Brother Stanley, would get buckets of mail but there was nothing for me. They did not commiserate with me but said, "Oh, your mail will come. Your mail will come." I kept saying to Brother Stanley, "Boy, no wonder, you're so victorious; you get everything your way. Everything works out right for you and nothing works out right for me and it makes me mad that you stand up there and you're so victorious." I said, "I wish somebody could get you mad. Why don't you just lose your temper with me?"

He did get mad once, and I could see that he is human. He's got a weak spot, but you know something, we all do. Our problem is that we are always hammering at the other guy's weak spot instead of comforting him or loving them and helping them out. It's not very Christian to go around bugging people and getting a kick out of the fact that you can get under their skin.

That was just the devil in me once again, trying to game and punish the other person because everything wasn't going right with me. That's real emotional immaturity. When you want to lash out at somebody else because everything isn't going right in your spiritual life that is real spiritual immaturity.

Another thing that bothered me on this trip is that I hated everything I had to eat. There was awful stuff. Raw fish and things... just swimming around, you didn't know what it was. Alive, dead, you couldn't dare ask. You wouldn't eat it if you did know what it was.

Every time we'd sit down at the table, Brother Stanley would say to Tom and me, "Now you kids can't sit together because you are bad influences on each other. None of you like to eat the food you are offered. These people have worked hard. They fix the best they have and you come to the meal and turn up your nose at it. How would you like it if you were entertaining company and you'd spent all day long cooking, and a lot of money gathering food for others and the guests come in and say, "I don't like that." "That's the height of ill manners," and he said, "I'm going to teach you a new song."

"Where He leads me, I will follow. What He feeds me, I will swallow," and he said, "Now you sit down and you eat," While I did not sing that song at the beginning of my time in Japan: by the last day my appreciation for my interpreter was so strong that out of love for him, I ate every single thing that was on my plate and I really enjoyed all of it. I wasn't doing it because I had to but because I did not want to insult his people nor did I want his people to think that my Jesus wasn't strong enough to give me victory over these things that were little things, perhaps for others, but they were great big things to me.

It was so wonderful one day when the hostess fixed all of this Japanese food and I really enjoyed it and the love that shown from her face when she saw that I really loved it was worth more than a thousand of my sermons on love. My victory did come out of a defeat.

Now I'd been having temper tantrums and I wanted to go home and Brother Stanley said I just was having a fit, but I really did want to go home. I didn't want to go to Korea, I'd had it and he said, "You can't go home, for your own sake, you can't go home." I said, "You're just like Saint Paul, the way he treated John Mark. I don't blame John Mark for leaving him. You're just like him. You're hard. You have no feelings."

I continued, "I've been with you men so long, I just can't stand it anymore. I want to talk to a woman. You think like men and you act like men and I want to be with women. I'm sick and tired of men. I want to be with women. I want to go home," but he wouldn't let me, and so I thought, "I'll just sulk and pout and act so ugly, that he will send me home." You know, he didn't, because he was mature and I was immature. He knew I was acting like a five year old kid and he thought, "I'll give her time now. She'll grow up."

He looked on my temper tantrums as a tempest in a teapot and he wasn't shaken as he knew that God was working on me. I said to Brother Stanley, "You're just like a concrete wall. Nobody can get through to you," and I said, "When you get to heaven, you'll be telling God what to do and He'll let you do it, too, because you've got that kind of influence in life. Everybody does what you want them to do."

> **Where He leads me, I will follow. What He feeds me, I will swallow.**

After saying all of these things to Brother Stanley, I had to go in and talk. I knew I wasn't ready to speak. How can you go from a temper tantrum into the pulpit and tell people about Jesus. You can't if you're looking at your own life. You can't, but if you look at Jesus, you can. I don't know how Jesus does it, but believe me He can make you an entirely different person.

I never knew what the grace of God was until I went to Japan and saw how in spite of my many bad reactions, it only brought out God's good reactions and the meaner I was, the better God was to me. God nearly killed me with His love and His love broke me. Every time I'd stand up to speak, I'd find people coming to see me. I thought, "Boy, if they only knew what a phony was standing in front of them. If I only had nerve enough to stand up and tell them what I'm really like, they'd be praying for me,

189

and they maybe could bring me to Jesus, and I could become the person I ought to be and wanted to be."

I recall one morning when I was so upset and so unhappy that I went into my room and I was in prayer for two hours before we all had to go to the closing session of the Ashram. I wasn't in victory, I was in defeat and I was one of the leaders, which made it even worse because that made me a phony.

I said to God, "I don't care if I get the victory. I'll go out of here in utter defeat, but let me be like Moses, Lord. Let me maybe not make the Promised Land at all. Maybe I'll never be happy. Maybe I'll never find what I'm looking for, but let me be like Moses. Let me help get all these other people in and shut the door and if they get in, that'll be enough for me. I don't have to have a victory. I don't even deserve it."

The Lord said to me, "When the Ashram closes, I'll close the door and they'll all be in, including you." On that final day of the Ashram, we had the Overflowing Heart. Everybody was shouting praises to God and describing the wonderful things that had happened to them, but one little girl stood up with tears running down her cheeks and said, "I have absolutely nothing. I'm going home with the same hate that I came with. I'm filled with hate and nothing has happened here at all to me."

I went over to her; I couldn't help it. I was so broken myself and I put my arms around her and I said, "Kneel down here with me." I don't know if she could even understand what I said. The interpreter was trying to tell her and I said, "The Lord Jesus promised me this morning that everybody was going to receive victory today and I was "going in" as well and I'm going to be the last one to get in, so I know that you're going too," and you know something, the Lord just quickened her and she received victory and she burst into song. She was just thrilled because the Lord touched her, but not because I stood above her and said, "I'm victorious and you're not." Instead, I had just knelt down next to her and said, "I'm just exactly like you, even worse than you are, and God said, "You are going in." My friend, you can't win people to Christ if you're thinking that you are too good. You don't know what people go through when their hearts are broken. You can't talk to a person if you don't talk from experience and how are you going to talk from experience if experiences – even the negative ones, don't happen to you.

The love of God is so wonderful that if He dared to show it to us directly you would just disintegrate. You couldn't bear to know how wonderful it is, but I learned the definition of grace on that trip to Japan. I had said to the Lord, "Lord, how can You send me from a temper tantrum into the pulpit and have this victory be the result. The worse I am to You, the better You are to me. How come?"

I then said to the Lord, "Every other place I'd been, the meaner I am, the meaner people are to me, I guess that's justified. If I am good, they're good. If I'm bad, they're bad, but not with You," and He said, "Mary, grace is the power of God to take the stubborn rebellion in a person and in a moment through the power of love to make it into willing cooperation. That's grace." How God does it, I don't know. How can you be one minute one way and then in the flash of a miracle another person entirely. I don't know, but something happens when you

191

meet Jesus Christ and the love of God starts operating in your life and He turns the terrible tragedies of our lives into Easter mornings.

He turns defeat into victory. Now Jesus Christ didn't say, "Repent or you'll go to hell." A lot of people preach that kind of a gospel, but what Jesus says is "Repent for the Kingdom of God is at hand." Give up the old and take the new because if your hands are full of the old, you can't hold the new and the new is a blessing. The victory comes out of defeat.

In thinking about the love of God, I was reminded of an occurrence with my oldest son, Ted. When he was in the fifth grade, his father was killed and it was a very hard and very emotional time for him. He wasn't hurt physically, but emotionally he was wounded. His whole world disintegrated because he loved his father so very much and it affected his schoolwork. He had been an average student but after his father's death doing well in the fifth grade became an impossible thing for him.

At the end of the year, he had a straight D average with some F's but the teacher loved him and so she passed him into the sixth grade. He came home at the end of school triumphant and said, "Mommy, I passed, I passed." Now you know, if I hadn't been a Christian, my pride would have said, "Thank God, he passed. I don't want to fail so my child can't fail," but I was a Christian and I saw my child, not as my child but as a boy whom God would use someday and I did not want him to be a failure, so I said to him, "Honey, come here a minute. Let's pray. Your grade card says that you passed into the sixth grade, but Teddy, what does your heart say? Did you really pass?"

You know what he said to me, "Momma, that's not fair, what'd you ask me that for?" He knew he hadn't passed. He knew that his teacher was trying to do him a favor. He knew that the fifth grade had been too hard for him and his teacher wanted him to go on, but it would have been in defeat, into the next grade and then the next grade and so I said, "Son, if you do that, by the time you get to the eighth grade, you will be so defeated and feel so humiliated, you'll quit school."

I continued, "When did they pass a law that you have to be a certain age to get out of a certain grade? You don't go to school for A's or B's, you go to school to learn. If you've really learned and you've got a straight D average, honey, praise the Lord, go on, but if you haven't really done so, son, pray about it and get victory enough in your soul that you won't be a defeatist. You won't just quit." "Because, son, it doesn't matter if you get to be 55 years old, if you don't conquer this time where you fell down, if you ignore it and pretend that it didn't happen, you will become emotionally insecure and I'm not interested in when you get out of school. I'm only interested in your life."

I said, "Honey, you know weavers create rugs and fabric by hand. A good weaver is really an artist. If, even

> **The grace of God is the most tremendous thing in the world and many of us don't even realize or appreciate its power and love until you really need it.**

after the weaving is almost done, the weaver sees a flaw, then a good weaver would tear it all out and go back to correct the flaw before he goes on. The imperfect weaver, who is only interested in what he will be paid rather than the quality of his workmanship, just pretends the flaw isn't there, but when the cloth comes to the marketplace, it's marked imperfect, second best." I said, "Son, I don't want your life to be marked second best. I want you to have first class everything because I love you. Now go to Jesus, pray about it. "Are you afraid the kids are going to laugh at you? Laugh at them first and beat them to punch, but don't give up in defeat." "The only time you're a failure is when you quit trying and you give up." "Jesus can make you a success, honey. If you can go back to where you fell down and conquer it then you can rise up out of that a new man." I said, "You pray about it." I went to the teacher and talked to her, you know what she said to me, "You're a funny kind of a mother. Don't you love your child? Any other mother would be coming in here wringing my neck if I were not going to let their child move to the next grade. I said, "I know but I'm not proud. I'm not on trial. My child's whole life is at stake and I'm a Christian."

Teddy came down the next morning and he said, "Ma, I'm going up and tell my teacher that I'm going to take fifth grade over." I said, "You want me to go with you?" and he said, "No, the Lord Jesus will go with me. He'll help me," and he said, "I don't care if the kids laugh at me. I'll laugh with them. It's kind of funny. I'll be a lot smarter next year because I already know most of the answers. I need help on some of them but the majority of it isn't going to be a struggle."

194

You know that the next year, that child earned a straight B average and on the inside of him, he had victory written over the defeat of the last year and, my friends, that's the kind of victory that Jesus wants to give us. Out of the ashes of the old comes this new thing that Jesus wants to give us.

Out of the ashes of the old comes the victory of the Lord Jesus. If you've got a problem this morning, take heart. You couldn't have been any more mixed up and messed up than I was in Japan and Korea. You couldn't have been more emotionally unstable or insecure than I was, nobody could be any worse. I hit bottom, but I tell you today I'm not that person any more, for Jesus makes the difference. I wouldn't be fair to you to stand up here and make you think that I'm a saint when I'm not. I'm a ransomed sinner saved by grace, just like you are if you've accepted Jesus Christ into your life.

My friend, you can't win people to Christ if you're thinking that you are too good. You don't know what people go through when their hearts are broken.

I want you to take heart this morning. You don't have a problem too big for the Son of God to handle and if you'll just turn it over to Him, turn your broken, mixed up, bankrupt life over to Him and you know what will happen? Your life will be transformed. You will be open for business under new management. That's right, if you give this old bankrupt life to Jesus Christ He will come in as the Efficiency Expert to put the old business under new management and your life will work.

This is the way to live. Turn your defeats over to Him and let Him give you victory. It's His victory that you're seeking not your own. If you could do it in your own strength, if you could control your own temper and control your own tongue, if you could quit all the bad habits that you had, you wouldn't need Jesus. However, that is not the case for us. You never outgrow your need for Jesus Christ. You'll always need a Savior.

When the Spirit of the Lord is speaking to you in that still, small voice, telling you to do something, don't argue with Him, just do it. It doesn't take long to not listen, just a second and the devil is waiting. Let's rejoice this morning for the good news is that Jesus is Lord!

Let God do something new in our hearts. My prayer was in Korea, "Oh, God, put me in a winepress and squeeze the me out of me so that I can be like You. I don't want this me in me. It gets me into all sorts of trouble. Take me and grind me up, Lord, like the bread and the wine. Crush me. Crucify me." You know what Jesus said to me, "Where do you think you are?"

Where do you think you are? We're in the gristmill and God's trying to make the communion elements out of us, the bread and the wine. The broken bread, the poured out wine to go out and save people and He can do it if we let Him. Take heart today and follow Him.

Shall we pray?

Lord Jesus, without You we're sunk. We can't do anything and the most profound statement we can make is when we say, "Lord, I can do nothing alone. I need you in my life. Help us to give ourselves to you and not hold anything back. Your blessing us at this Ashram will enable us to be a blessing to someone else. Thank You, Jesus. Amen.

E. Stanley Jones and Mary Webster in Tokyo

FIVE

WHOSE RIGHTS REALLY MATTER?

INTRODUCTION

Surrender to God is not merely about giving up darkness, it is also about giving in to light and it is about giving up our "rights" in love.

> I learned, when I met Jesus, to surrender my life and to the degree that I was able to do that, I've had a perfectly wonderful time getting along with people. However, every single time I took back that surrender, and insisted on my "rights," I found that I became undone and was in trouble all over again.

Mary's initial acceptance of God into her life was only the beginning of the transformations to come. Mary found that this love of Christ she had invited into her life demanded expression. For her the simplest and most ordinary of things became acts of love when she performed them in awareness and gratitude for the love of God shining within her. Her "rights" were not relevant to the expression of love. And so it can be with all of us. All of life becomes our spiritual practice when we live and work and serve others as a response to God's so freely available love.

Read how Mary's relationships dramatically changed when she gave up her rights.

My whole life became sacramental. I wasn't just doing something spiritual and saintly on Sunday morning; I was doing every little thing in a sacramental manner all day long.

I WOULD LIKE TO SHARE with you tonight something that I think is important in our everyday lives and certainly in our Christian experience. And this is just a matter of our rights. I heard as a young bride that I had rights in my marriage and that I should only give up 50% of my rights. I was advised not to do too much for a man, so that he can do something for me. And as long as I followed that guidance I had a terrible time being happily married. But when Jesus came and I surrendered my life, I found that I loved my husband 100% for nothing. I didn't love him because of the washing machine he gave me, or the dryer, or the clothes, or the money, or the house, or anything.

I loved him for nothing. And for a long time I loved God because he gave me this and he gave me that and he did this and he did that for me. But I learned, when I met Jesus, to surrender my life and to the degree that I was able to do that, I've had a perfectly wonderful time getting along with people. But every single time I reach out and take back that surrender, and insist on my "rights" I find that I become undone and am in trouble. And so tonight, I would like to share with you some illustrations about how God has helped me in this particular area.

I recall telling you previously the story about my girlfriend and the rhubarb. This friend would come to my house and spend lots of time with me, really too much time. She also began to think that everything that I did was just perfect and she gave me personal credit for everything that Jesus had done for me. And of course, that began to worry me because I was becoming an idol to her. She wasn't able to go to Jesus through me, rather she was coming to me and stopping there. I could see that she was going to be in worse shape if she continued to idolize me and not focus on Jesus.

So I prayed and I said, "Jesus, how can I help this girl focus her eyes on You and keep them there? How can I help her to see that to the degree that I am surrendered to you, I am happy. How can I help her see that it's You who is making the difference in my life. I am not perfect and do not deserve all the credit that she gives me." And the Lord told me a very simple way to show her.

This is what happened. She was spending the weekend again with me and I got up one morning and went down to get breakfast. When she came downstairs a while later, I said to her, "You know Jane, you think that my sister-in-law and I are two angels and that's why we get along together, and you think that it's because your father is so awful that that's why you don't get along with him but I want you to know that neither Aunt May nor I are angels. However, I'm a Christian and she's a Christian and that's what makes all the difference in our home life."

"All we do is try to make each other happy. But for an hour this morning, I'm going to do something and I want you to understand what I'm doing. For one hour this morning, I'm not going to do anything patently un-Christian but I'm going to take back my rights and exert them." And I added, "Now Jane, you know that ever since I've lived in the house with Aunt May, every single morning when she gets up and comes into the room, I'm already there. I'm always the first one to speak and say, 'Good morning, how are you?' Well, today I'm tired of doing that. I've done it for so many years, it looks to me like she ought to speak first just one morning. So this is that morning, I'm not going to speak to her if she doesn't speak to me. Now I'm not mad at her or anything and I think she's tremendous, but if she doesn't speak to me first I'm not going to speak to her. I'm going to see how long she can go without initiating a conversation. Let's just see what will happen. Watch closely.

All I did, my friends, was to plant a little seed of doubt in Jane's mind. I got her to be suspicious. And it didn't take long for the tension to mount. My sister-in-law came into the kitchen and I just stood

"Jesus, how can I help this girl focus her eyes on You and keep them there? How can I help her to see that to the degree that I am surrendered to you, I am happy."

there looking at her, waiting for her to say something. She didn't understand what was the matter and I suppose she thought that Jane and I wanted to be alone because she went on through the kitchen to the bathroom and didn't say anything.

Jane said to me, "What's the matter with her, anyway?" Jane never would have had that thought if I hadn't created an atmosphere of suspicion. Many times, our trouble lies in just the fact that we don't have to do anything directly unkind, we can just be the catalytic agent that gets suspicion and tension started and we can sit back and watch it grow. And now Jane, who never before thought ill of Aunt May was now suspicious. And so the tension began to build, just a little bit of it at first, but as Aunt May started back through the kitchen to her bedroom she looked at us and must have thought it odd that we didn't even speak to her. When she was out of hearing, Jane said to me, "What's the matter with that woman?" I said, "I don't know, that's the way she always is. I always have to speak first."

Then the telephone rang, and usually when someone calls my sister-in-law, who is disabled, I like to answer the calls to help her out. But instead of doing that, I said to Jane, "You know, I always take her calls and handle them and it takes so much of my time and I'm busy this morning. And I'm just going to let Aunt May deal with her own phone calls. I haven't got time to be bothered with her this morning. I've got a right to sit and eat my breakfast for once and not be interrupted." So I went to the telephone and I picked it up and it was Jenny and she wanted Aunt May to go to a party in the afternoon. Now I knew this was probably why she called. Jenny asked, "Is Aunt May up?" And I said, "Just a minute, I'll call her."

I yelled out, "Aunt May, telephone!" Well I suppose Aunt May wondered what in the world was the matter with me this morning, I didn't speak to her and now I'm yelling at her to come to the phone. Why wouldn't I take a message for her? I could hear Aunt May getting mad. I could hear her trying to hurry, and you know when you're trying to hurry you do things too quickly and drop things. And the more Aunt May tried to hurry, the madder she got. Finally, when she got to the telephone, she yelled, "Hello!" And I suppose Jenny, on the other end, thought what in the world's got into her and what is she so mad about?

Well, in the course of their phone conversation, I could hear Aunt May saying, very loudly for my benefit no doubt, because she thought if I overheard her conversation, I would certainly volunteer my services for the day, like I usually did. So I rattled the dishes on the table to make her think that I didn't hear, and that made her even madder. She was saying to Jenny, "Well, I'm very sorry. Mary's got company this afternoon and I'm disabled and I don't have any way to get around and I just won't be able to go with you and besides, my hair's not fixed." And wham she slammed down the phone receiver.

I imagine Jenny turned to Arlene, her daughter-in-law, and said, "Well! May can't go to the party and I can't go either." I imagine that's what happened because that's the way it goes, each guy passes the frustration on to the next person who doesn't deserve it. Well, Aunt May hobbled back into the bedroom and she must have been getting to the boiling point by this time. My overt behavior was sweet and kind, and Christians can be so kind when they're dishing it out and not having to take it.

I was very sweet and kind and I said to Jane, "You know, it just dawned on me that every single morning since I've been married and lived in this house, I get up and prepare the breakfast and then when Aunt May comes in I say to her, "Aunt May, would you like a hard boiled egg or a soft boiled egg or a poached egg or a fried egg? Now would you like toast or would you like biscuits? Would you like shredded wheat or would you like corn flakes?"

I said, "But today, if she doesn't like what I've got on the table this morning, she can get her own breakfast. I'm sick and tired of making her whatever she wants for breakfast. What is the sense of it anyway? Nobody does this for me." Well now I could see Jane was getting uncomfortable because the tension by this time had mounted considerably. Rather than wait for Aunt May to join us for breakfast like we usually did, we just sat down and started to eat. I said, "I just want to eat one hot meal. I never get a good hot meal, I always have to jump up and down and wait on everybody, or wait until they get to the table, so I'm going to go ahead and eat. "So we were eating and when Aunt May came in; she plopped down in her chair and said, "Please pass the sugar."

Without being sweet and passing the sugar gently to her I just slid it across the table as if I were in a hurry and wanted to convey to her my "busyness." Well, Aunt May ate her breakfast but she was getting madder and madder and Jane was getting more and more uncomfortable and nobody said anything. We were afraid to talk. We were afraid we'd explode. Now, tension is a powerful thing. You can't see it, but everybody feels it. And so Aunt May, to get away from this unseen enemy that she had run into this morning, finally got up from the table, excused herself and went out to tend her flower bed. There's something very consoling about pansy faces, they look up at you and they smile. And they don't look a thing like your relatives.

So she went out and looked at the little pansies and I started clearing off the dishes. Jane was watching Aunt May from the window and suddenly said, "Mary, come here quick!" I said, "Now what is she doing?" She said, "Why Mary, she's out here trying to pull the weeds out of the garden with her two crutches." I said, "Oh, Jane, she's just showing off. She doesn't have to do that. She could ask me and in a minute I could weed that flower bed. But if she's too proud to ask me then let her fall, I don't care."

Well, that did it. Jane whirled me around and shook me, and she was strong. She said, "You're a perfect little devil without Jesus Christ!" I said, "Why, Jane, it's taken you just one hour to make the biggest discovery of your life. That's the biggest truth you've ever said, that's exactly what I'd be without Jesus Christ. A perfect devil. I'm not a half-devil, I'm a perfect devil without Jesus Christ." And I said, "Jane, I'm going to show you something. You look back on it. Have I said one unkind or one un-Christian word to Aunt May this morning?"

Jane said, "No." I responded, "No, but I have provided an atmosphere in which the devil can work and he's had a wonderful time doing it. I haven't done anything or said anything unkind to her. But I haven't done anything good or kind or Christian, either. I've only created an atmosphere of unhappiness. And we've all had to live with it." Now I said, "You count on the clock how many minutes it takes me to pour the oil of Jesus Christ upon these troubled waters."

I went out to Aunt May and I said, "What are you trying to do, honey, break your neck?" "Now you tell me what you're weeding and I'd be more than glad to weed your garden for you." And I was soon down on my knees pulling up the weeds and the tension began to go down considerably. Then I said, "I thought you wanted to go to that party this afternoon." She said, "I did but I can't go. I don't have any way to go." I said, "Why you know that's why I'm here. I'm your chauffeur and if you want to go anywhere there's nothing I'd rather do this afternoon than to take you and Jenny to the party and come and pick you back up. Now you go on in the house and wash your hands and call her up and tell her we'll pick her up about quarter to one and we'll be more than glad to bring her back." And I added, "And by the way, get your curlers out and I'll fix your hair for you, okay?"

I gave her a kiss on the cheek and that woman went in singing. In five minutes of me surrendered to Jesus and letting him live through me, we had peace back in our family. I went back into the house and said to Jane, "Now Jane, why don't you go home and try this experiment with your father. You've always been fighting him, you think that he's wrong and everything he does is wrong. Why don't you go home in the power of Jesus Christ and just provide an atmosphere of Heaven for your father. It's worth it because you're going to live in it, too."

Well, Jane didn't say anything to me, but God pursued that idea directly with her. She went home and the first thing she did, was to prepare her father supper. She had his bath water all ready for him when he got home. She went out to the car, she carried in his briefcase, she kissed him, and told him how much she appreciated him. When he came in, the fellow thought his daughter had had a stroke. Jane had never acted like that before. She said, "Daddy, you go and take your bath and I have your supper all ready. Is there anything I can do to make you know how much I love you and appreciate you?" Her father started to cry. Jane began to live in an atmosphere of Heaven with her father as she surrendered to Christ.

Now, sadly shortly after this reconciliation, Jane's father died, and she was left alone. She had to go out and get a job and go to work. She was a brand new Christian and went to work in a factory where her boss was an un-Christian woman with a violent tongue and a vicious personality. However, Jane went up to her, full of Christian love and she said, "Well, I'm grateful that I'm going to get this job." And the woman just ripped her up and she said, "Well, you'll be fired in two weeks."

Jane said, "Well, what makes you say that?" She said, "No woman has ever worked for me for more than two weeks. I take delight in crucifying people. I hate people." She continued, "I'll just be so nasty to you that you'll quit on general principle." Jane said, "Well, don't you know that you can catch more bees with sugar than you can with vinegar?" The boss said, "Well, I don't get down on my knees to anybody."

Turn the love of God loose on them and they haven't got any arguments!

Jane went up to her and smiled. That's a dirty Christian trick to do to a person. Turn the love of God loose on them and they haven't got any arguments! And she said to her, "Well, that's why I'll be here when you're gone. Because I get down on my knees to somebody every night. And that habit makes it easy for me to get down on my knees to you." Jane continued, "You're an answer to prayer. You are an out and out answer to prayer. I'm a brand new Christian, and you know Christians can't grow around people who are good to them, they have to have somebody be mean to them. I've had plans to find somebody to just

209

treat me like I deserve so that I can show them what it is to be a Christian."

Jane continued, "You know, I wish you would just swear at me and treat me like I deserve, so I can show you what it means to be a Christian because this is what I've been praying for." The woman looked at her in amazement and said, "Well, if it'll make you so blankety blank happy, I won't do it!" And so Jane began to love her into the kingdom of God. Every time this woman would lash out at Jane, Jane would thank God. This was what she'd been waiting for, a chance to show a person what it means to be a Christian. That a Christian can take it because they have Jesus.

Jane's story reminded me of a Jewish boy who had just became a Christian and his friends persecuted him by following him home from school and threw rocks at him and called him filthy names. One night, to escape them, he ran into the sanctuary of the church. He was kneeling at the altar rail, praying that God would help him to love those people and not fight back. The boys who were taunting him followed him into the church and one of the boys doubled up his hands and while the little boy was bowed in prayer, just hit him as hard as he could right across the base of the neck. He said, "Take that for Jesus Christ."

The little boy put his hands up to his neck and as the pain hit him and the tears rolled down his cheeks, he smiled and said, "Thank you, I will." That's what it means to be a Christian. When you surrender. When you let them walk all over you, and you let them throw rocks at you, and you don't want to fight back, then you are fully surrendered to Christ. You're waiting for the opportunity to show a person who doesn't know that he's all mixed up inside that a Christian can take the worst that can comes to him. However, that won't happen without surrendering your "rights."

If we look at Jesus on the cross, we see that that's exactly what he did. He laid his rights down. He said we wouldn't have any power over him at all, except what was given to us. So the way to get rid of our enemies is to give them the opportunity to crucify us, if we know how to take it.

A friend of mine from the Texas Ashram came to me and said that she and her husband had been married for twelve years and they'd done nothing but fight ever since they'd been married. Each one wanted his or her own way. She said, "I tell you, we fight over everything. It doesn't matter what it is, we get in an argument over it." She said, "Well, Mary, I've just come to a point, after twelve years, I can't take anymore. And I want to get divorced." She said, "I've tried everything and I cannot get along with this man."

I said, "I don't think you've tried everything because I don't think you've tried Jesus." She got mad and said, "Now just what would you suggest that I do?" I said, "Well, honey, "I'd think twice before I threw a man out that you've lived with for twelve years." I said, "I think your pride's involved." She said, "Well, I'll have you know that I'm a Christian." I said, "That's wonderful, now you can go home and act like one. Surrender yourself. Go home and be a Christian to your husband. And if it doesn't work, you can always get a divorce. I'd try it, anyway. Because I think you love your husband. When you go home, Jewel, before you go home, go to the altar. Surrender your pride, your resentment, your rights. Just love your husband for nothing, just the way he is."

Jewel said, "But he's so egotistical!" and she started in on him again. I said, "Well, he's not your problem. Your problem is the way you react to who he is. Why don't you get his breakfast on Sunday morning. That'll get him, if nothing else." Typically she would go home from the Ashram and try to cram the Ashram into her husband who hadn't been to one. And you know that never works.

The more she threw up her religion to him, the more he threw it back up to her. He kept saying, "Well, if that's what it means to be a Christian, you can have it!" And that would make her furious. Every time she'd come home from a retreat he'd say to her, "Well, Miss High and Mighty, what did you get this time that won't work?" So, I told her, "Before you go home, this time surrender yourself to Jesus Christ. This thing in you that fights him, get rid of it. The only way you can get rid of it, is to read the crucifixion story over and over and over and over until you know that it was because of your attitude that Jesus died. And then I said, "Surrender yourself, and your rights, and then go home for Jesus' sake and ask your husband to forgive you. Admit that you're wrong and ask him to forgive you."

Jewel said, "Why, he'd laugh in my face." I continued, "All right, so what if he does? But at least try it. You've got nothing to lose and you've got everything to gain." She went to the altar and prayed, but I had a feeling that she was hoping that God would go to work on her husband, too. She didn't say it, but the tone of her voice almost made me feel like she was saying to God, "Well don't forget that he needs something as well."

I wondered if I had high-pressured her into this surrender. But a month later, when I opened a letter from her, I was so thrilled that I knelt down beside my bed and just thanked God. She said, "Mary, I wished you could have been there that Sunday morning when I got home from the Ashram. My husband came downstairs and when he saw that I had his breakfast ready, he nearly fainted. Because I never get up on Sunday morning and get his breakfast. And to keep from complimenting me for getting his breakfast, he sat down at the table and jerked his napkin out across his lap and said in that egotistical way he has in doing things, "Well, Miss High and Mighty, what did you get out of this retreat?"

She continued, "I was at the stove at the time and I had a skillet in my hand frying an egg. I just had an urge to go over there and wrap that thing around his neck and I remembered that's why Jesus had to die. That the urge to hurt, to hit, to fight back was only a symptom in me that I was very un-surrendered. The self in me still wanted to exert itself. And right then and there, I said, 'Oh, Jesus, save me.' And then a flood of love came into my heart for my husband. And before I even thought about it twice, I went over and knelt down beside him, of all things, on the kitchen floor, and I took his hands in mine and I said, 'I know that I'm the reason that we don't get along and I want you to know that I'm sorry. I didn't mean to irritate you, but I wasn't a Christian and Jesus is going to help me now, if you'll give me another chance. I want to be a Christian wife to you. Let's don't get a divorce. Let me live this way for a little while and see if it works. Please give me another chance.'"

213

Jewel continued, "Well, Mary, he almost knocked the dishes off the table. He got down on his knees beside me and took me in his arms and kissed me and said, "For twelve years, honey, I've been trying to say I'm sorry but you wouldn't let me. That attitude of yours made it impossible. I wanted to hit back instead of loving you. And look at all the time we've wasted when we could have been in each other's arms."

She wrote, "We found Christ on our knees, beside our table in the kitchen. And we found each other for the first time in twelve years, we were one. We weren't two people fighting for superiority, we were a couple, which we should have been all along. And we dedicated ourselves to go out and find other broken marriages and homes and help those people go to the foot of the cross, together. Mary, we know that unhappily married couples put on this big act and we can see right through it. We did it. When we surrender, something wonderful happens in each person. We don't think it will but we never know unless we try that it really works."

Now I had an experience that is related to this message. When my sister-in-law came home from the hospital, she was still a semi-invalid and I had to bathe her and help her with a bedpan. This wasn't something I was trained to do and at first I didn't mind it, I mean, I loved her and while I didn't exactly like to give her a bath and empty the bedpan, I did it because... Well, I just didn't think of anything else to do. The trouble was, that when other Christian people and non-Christian people came to our house they were "struck" by what I was doing. They began to talk about how nice it was for me to care so beautifully for Aunt May and they made those comments in front of me. Did you ever tell a little child she was beautiful and the first thing you know she's looking in the mirror and believing it.

Well I could hear them talking about me as I left the room, "My, isn't it wonderful that Mary is sacrificing her life waiting on this woman. She doesn't have to, most of her relatives wouldn't do it. Isn't she a wonderful Christian?" Each time I pretended it didn't bother me and I'd go back in, and you know there's such an old "ham" in me that I would begin to "act" like a Christian instead of being one. The funny thing about acting like a Christian is when your audience leaves you don't want to act anymore. And then you begin to react.

We found Christ on our knees, beside our table in the kitchen. And we found each other for the first time in twelve years, we were one. We weren't two people fighting for superiority, we were a couple, which we should have been all along.

Now God knew this about me and this is a wonderful thing about Jesus. He's a total savior. He's not going to do a halfway job of salvation, He's going to come into every single area that's wrong and He's going to keep His light on it until we see it as sin and then we ask Him to cleanse it. And I love what Brother Tom said, "Jesus Christ will never cleanse you from your nerves, if you call it nerves, but if you call it temper or sin, He'll cleanse you from that." He said that people who've been in the church for

215

fifty years aren't any further along spiritually than the day they got here because they don't call a sin a sin.

So the Lord knew this "act" was sin in me, but I didn't know it. I wasn't even aware of it consciously. So one night I walked through the bedroom to give my sister-in-law the bedpan and when I took it back into the bathroom to empty it I got down on my knees and I was honest to God, and I said, "All right, Lord, I'm here. I can't do this anymore! I don't like to do it! I wasn't cut out to do this! Give me a job that I was made to do. But don't make me empty bedpans. I don't like it. I don't want to give baths to people either. I'll do something big, I'll preach sermons for you but don't make me do this because this isn't something I like to do." I wanted to do something spiritual.

I was honest with God. The one thing about sin is if you get it up and get it out then God will help. Jesus said to me, "Mary, I know that you don't like to do this. I know you've never liked to do it. But I want you to know something. You tell me how every time you wash your sister-in-law's leg that's injured, you always tell me how thankful you are that you have two good legs. Well, Mary, I can't believe that kind of a prayer. The only way I'll ever know that you appreciate your legs and the ability to walk is when you go, in my Name, out of gratitude to me, and help somebody who can't walk. Then I'll know that you do appreciate your legs. But if you're just going to send up repetitious "gratitude" to me and call that prayer, it isn't really prayer because I know you don't really mean it."

So I said, "Lord, I'm so sorry. What am I going to do? I love her, I want to help her, but I don't want to do this." He said, "I know you don't. But I do. I came into the world to help people who couldn't help themselves and I never get tired of it. It never bothers me, it never irritates me, I don't care how dirty the job is. I never mind it. Mary, I want to help her. You're the only hands and feet I have to do it with. Couldn't you do it please?"

You know, I realized in the flash of an instant what Jesus meant. The words across the communion table in our church read, "Do this in remembrance of me." And when I take communion in such of a lovely atmosphere, I feel that God and I are really connected. It is all so beautiful and tidy. But Jesus was saying to me, "If you want to commune with me, empty that bedpan in remembrance of me. Do it in remembrance of me. Don't do it for her sake, don't do it for your sake. Do it for My sake."

And He said to me, "Do you remember the story of the king who said to those on his right hand, "Come in, I've prepared a place for you, for I was hungry and you fed me, I was thirsty and you gave me drink, I was in prison and you visited me. I was sick and you came to me. And as much as you did it unto the least of these you did it unto Me. And those who didn't do it for others didn't do it for me." He continued, "Mary, which one are you?"

I said, "Lord, please forgive me. I want to help Aunt May. I love her. And I do want to do it for you." And the Lord said, "All right, Mary, it's not your duty to do it. It's a sacred privilege. For in as much as you do it for her, you're doing it for Me, there's only one way you can show me you love Me. Just do it for her and I'll know you're doing it for Me."

So I went back into the bedroom and I was so broken-hearted I could hardly keep the tears back. I thought, oh, if my sister-in-law knew what I was going through in that bedroom. She didn't ask to be disabled, she doesn't like to be at somebody's mercy. She thinks I love her, and I'm a hypocrite. When I went back into the room, I said to her, "Aunt May, would you like me to give you a back rub tonight after I give you a bath?" I'd never volunteered to do that before. I simply did what I was required to do but nothing else.

She said, "Well, Mary you have so many things to do and you're so tired, I wouldn't want to add to your burden, but if you would like to give me a back rub I would deeply appreciate it because I get so tired lying here all day long, and the muscles in my back ache." I said, "All right, I'll give you a back rub." So I began to put alcohol on her back, and I was rubbing her back. She said to me, "Mary, you have the touch of an angel. When the nurses do it, they are in a hurry to get done, I can tell. But you do it as if you really love me. You want me to be comfortable."

By then the tears were just streaming down my cheeks, I couldn't stand it but I couldn't put my hands up to wipe them because I had alcohol on them. I was in agony, because I knew what I had done. I knew that it wasn't me that was giving May a back rub, it was Jesus in me. I had admitted that I didn't want to give May a back rub at all. But Jesus did. As I looked at my hands, I saw they were not my hands, they were His hands. I had loaned them to Him. And He was doing it, not me. As I looked at her body I realized that it was not her body, it was His. And I could scarcely stand to be in that room, it was so full of Jesus.

Jesus taught me what it meant to really take communion. "Do this in remembrance of Me." I got so that when

I'd go into the grocery store I'd hear those words, 'Do this in remembrance of me,' and if I had one article and a woman came with a whole big basket full of groceries, I'd say, "Be my guest. Go ahead of me." I won't shove and push anymore. It's a privilege to let you go ahead of me because as much as I do it to you, I do it unto Him.

My whole life began to become sacramental, it wasn't just doing something on Sunday morning, it was doing everything all day long. And every single time I hurt a

> My whole life began to become sacramental, it wasn't just doing something on Sunday morning, it was doing every little thing all day long... Every time I did something that brought a smile to someone else's face, I knew that I had made Jesus smile.

person I could hear something inside of me just pounding the nails into His feet. Every time I did something that brought a smile to someone else's face, I knew that I had made Jesus smile. And it was not even me that did it, but Jesus living in me. So I learned that communion is not something carved across a wooden table, but when Jesus Christ carves across your heart, 'Do this in remembrance of Me', this is the greatest blessing. You don't do it for somebody, you don't do it for money, you do it for Jesus.

Now in closing, I'd like for you to bow your head and close your eyes and think about Jesus. Think about your own life and the people you live with and the atmosphere in your family. I would like to share a portion of the vision of Sir Lancelot. You may remember this story. This knight from King Arthur's court had spent his whole life seeking the Holy Grail, the cup that Jesus drank from at the last supper. He thought if he could possess the cup, something wonderful would happen in his life. So, foolishly, he set out upon a journey, seeking, seeking, seeking for the Holy Grail. The wonderful cup that Jesus had touched.

But he never found the Holy Grail and in his discouragement he started back home. As he was walking along the road leading his horse, he heard an old man crying, 'Give me a drink of water. Give me a drink of water.' He picked up the old man in his arms and went to his saddle bag and got out his own cup. He knelt down beside the stream and got a cup of cold water. Then he tenderly lifted the old man up in his arms again and put the cup of water to his lips. As he did, you remember, the Lord Jesus appeared to him and said, "The Holy supper is kept in these. In what we share with another's need. It's not what we give, it's what we share. For the gift without the giver is bare. Who gives himself with his gift, sees straight. Himself, his hungry neighbor, in Me."

Oh, Lord Jesus, tonight as we go home from this Ashram if there's one thing we could do, if we could just come and be healed, spiritually, physically, emotionally, so that we might go home and prepare an atmosphere in which our family, the ones we live with, could find it easy to be a Christian and to remain a Christian, and to love each other as unto Thee. Help us, Lord, to learn this wonderful secret, to provide a Heaven for someone else, and then we know that we, too, are experiencing the same Heaven that you have prepared for someone else through us.

As we come to the altar tonight in prayer, we pray that we will not seek the kingdom. That we will want the kingdom. That we don't want the gift, we want the giver. Help us tonight, dear Father, to know that we would rather have wholeness than healing and that if we're touched by Jesus spiritually, and made whole inwardly, it doesn't matter anymore whether we're physically whole or well or not. That the greatest healing that can come to us is when our hearts are right with God and when we are living for the sake of God. Our lives have been surrendered and others who see our good works will give glory to our Father who is in Heaven. And now bless us and keep us and prepare our hearts for the sermon that is to follow. We ask in the name of the Father and the Son and the Holy Spirit, Amen.

Mary Webster and other in 1970s

SIX

GROWING

IN

LOVE

INTRODUCTION

In this talk Mary discovers there's a great difference between merely saying the word "love" to somebody and really and truly loving them the way God wants us to love. To love, not in word, but in truth, is where love is expressed in deed as a byproduct of love. Mary admonishes us never to count the cost of loving, but to love God and our neighbors for nothing. She affirms this message because she has dramatically experienced the essence of God as love.

Mary shares how we can attune our ears to the SOS of humankind through a series of moving illustrations: a hotel manager whose relationships are fraught with anger and hostility, an alcoholic husband, a moving mother's day message from Mary's eldest son, a little bee, and Helen, who initially did not experience that Christians are people who care. Mary cautions patience in this process, for love has an inspired vision of perfecting everyone. This is because it looks to the future, and the unseen, with joy and anticipation for good.

Love is willing to wait forever. It has the touch of the eternal upon it and love has the ability to take whatever comes without wavering or doubting or looking back but instead goes full steam ahead to the future, facing whatever lies ahead, with whatever lies at hand to engage others in the experience of the Word become Flesh... love put into action.

1ST JOHN 3:18, READS, "My little children, let us not love in word or tongue but in deed and in truth." I would like to talk tonight about the love of God as I have experienced it over the last few months. This new experience of the love of God in works and deeds has been transformational.

One day, I was in a hospital with a nurse who was attending a patient with cancer and I wanted to go in the room with her to pray for the patient and talk to him about Jesus. I thought to myself, I love people and I thought, "I'm in a hospital now. I'll go in and I'll love these people for Jesus' sake."

The only problem was that I was not prepared to witness the physical devastation that cancer caused this patient and as the nurse took the bandages off, I forgot all about talking to this person about Jesus. I forgot all about anything because I became dizzy and left the room to keep from fainting.

When the nurse finished the care of her patient, she asked me "What was the matter with you?" I said, "I know one thing, I could never be a nurse." She looked at me strangely and she said, "Why?" I said, "Because I just can't stand to see people suffer like that." Then she looked at me even more strangely and she said, "Isn't that strange? That's the reason I am a nurse because I can't stand to see people suffer and I want to do something about it."

I realized that I had the word love become only a word but she had the word love become flesh and rolled up her

225

sleeves and went out doing something about human suffering through love.

My friends, I've discovered there's a great difference in just saying the word love to somebody and really and truly loving them the way God wants us to love, not in word, but in truth, where love is expressed in deed as a byproduct of love.

Last summer, a group of us went to Hawaii to hold an Ashram. One of our leaders said that she was led by the Lord to hold the Ashram in a specific hotel. When we got to the hotel, the manager was drunk and he was verbally abusing his wife in a way that was horrifying. It was just awful.

We took a room near the office because we thought that the quarreling between the manager and his wife would not bother us. However, at about 2 in the morning, my roommate, (the one, who said that the Lord led her to this hotel), was suddenly awakened and heard the verbal abuse. I could see that she was suffering and told me the devil said to her, "God sent you here? This is a wonderful place to hold an Ashram, just listen to what's going on."

I tried my best to pretend that I was asleep and couldn't hear the conversation between the manager and his wife. I wanted to drown out the man's words and did not want them to go through my mind and end up in my subconscious. As I was lying there I heard Jesus saying to Peter and John and the other Disciples, when He was in the garden, "Could you not watch and wait even one hour?"

My friends, I received a tremendous revelation from God as I was lying there. I'd been brought up in a wonderful atmosphere, I had everything under the sun that I ought to have to be happy and here's a man whose soul was in hell and he was sending out an SOS. "Help me. Can't you see, there's something wrong with me? You're a Christian, save me," and what did I do? I wanted him to shut up so I could go back to sleep and so I tried to ignore his distress message, but to my peril.

It never occurred to me to get on my knees and start to pray for this man and so Jesus said to me, "Can't you even wait and watch one hour? This is just one man's face. This is the evil in one man you're listening to, but I have to listen to all the evil in all the people in the entire world all the time, 24 hours a day, I can't sleep. I have to listen to it constantly and it's killing me and I was put on the cross to stop it. Why don't you do something about it? Of course I led your roommate to this hotel. This man needs what you've got more than anyone else in Hawaii."

> I realized that I had the word love become only a word but she had the word love become flesh and rolled up her sleeves and went out doing something about suffering through love.

Believe me, it wasn't long before I was on my knees as well and I went over to my roommate and said, "The devil's telling you that God didn't send you here, isn't he? God did send us here. Let's be an Ashram to this man. Let's give him the love of God, instead of pulling out tomorrow morning because the atmosphere isn't conducive to worship. Let's make it conducive to worship," and so we did.

The next morning, there wasn't a single Christian in our group who complained to that manager. We didn't leave the hotel. We just pulled up closer to Jesus and let Jesus shine through us. The next morning, very early, the song leader was out by the swimming pool singing about Jesus and as the manager woke out of his drunken stupor he said, "That man can wake me up any morning singing like that..." Our song leader was singing "No One Ever Cared for Me Like Jesus."

On Thursday evening the manager of the hotel allowed us, imagine, he allowed us to have a party at the hotel. In Hawaii, leis of flowers are given to everyone whom you love. We'd invited half of the island to come, free of charge, to be our guests, and the manager furnished us the most beautiful supper and he had his arm around his wife most of the time. He invited all the guests of the hotel to come to the party and he asked me to give my witness to all those people.

The most wonderful thing that I've ever seen was to see that man and his wife together again. While he did not accept Jesus into his life that night, three others did. They said to me, "Look, we came to Hawaii to have a good time. We didn't know we were going to run into God here," but God had led them to that hotel, as well.

We learned that if you're going to be an Ashram, you've got to be the Word become Flesh and you can't wait for a convenient hour to go out and witness to others, rather you have to have your ear tuned, your spiritual ear tuned to the SOS of humankind.

When a person is saying (even without words but through actions) "I need help. Save me," and I don't hear his communication then I miss his SOS. I was so embarrassed and so ashamed because I realize that it is so easy to say, "I love people. I'm going out and help people. I'm going to Hawaii, to tell people about Jesus," and when the first person I meet who really needs to know the Lord, I run away and hide.

I don't think that I had ever really seen God's love quite like I did that night in Hawaii. The only reason I was able to respond to the manager's SOS was because God's great Spirit moved me to put my general love into specific action. There's no difference between me and that man except Jesus Christ and so I've been writing to him and witnessing to him and I pray that someday that man will know that Jesus Christ loves him just as much as Jesus loves me.

As I was thinking about the love of God I have been re-reading the 13th chapter of First Corinthians every morning during the Ashram. As I was reading the chapter, I wrote down some insights that came to me and I would like to share them with you.

Love does not feel slighted or hurt at every little thing that occurs nor feel badly when others receive honors it is denied. Love does not fawn on others or promote its own influence and accomplishments, rather love forgets its own self by becoming lost in the interests of others and their accomplishments. Love does not always listen for the sound of its own voice but it listens and learns from the voices of others.

Love does not push its weight around neither contradict nor delight in exhibiting the mistakes of others but love takes into its own heart all those mistakes and hurts and holds them close. Love does not pout and sulk if its plans are upset but it enters cheerfully into the situation and helps rescue some good from it. Love does not have to be handled with kid gloves. It doesn't get irritated over trifles or act high and mighty.

Love doesn't have a chip on its shoulder. Love doesn't read self into everything and therefore love does not perceive slights. Love does not get secret pleasure from seeing harm or evil come to others. It overcomes evil with love and goodwill. Love calls out the highest from the very lowest and believes that "highest" into being. Love is sacrificial for it embodies the hurts of others, gladly. It is grateful that it has been privileged to be able to spare another person's hurt feelings. Love is honest and open. Therefore Love trusts and believes the best about everything in everybody.

Love has an inspired vision of perfecting everyone for it looks to the future and to the unseen with joy and anticipation for good. Finally, love is willing to wait forever. It has the touch of the eternal upon it and love has the ability to take whatever comes without wavering or doubting or looking back but instead goes full steam ahead into the future, facing whatever lies ahead, with whatever lies at hand to engage others in the experience of the Word become Flesh which is love put into action.

This is the sort of Love that God offered me when I prayed for the hotel manager in Hawaii. Unfortunately many of us who affirm that Jesus is love do not illustrate that love in our interactions with others. We often hurt one another, and while we don't mean to do so, we do.

I remember one morning, I was praying and thinking of all the little boys and girls that I had in Sunday school, little wiggly boys and girls who find it so very difficult to sit still and listen to anything.

I found that as I prayed for each of those children, five, 10, 15 minutes at a time that I began to see in them the face of Jesus. As I sat in silence and just looked into His eyes, something transformative occurred. Let me illustrate. As I left the prayer room later, I saw a little honeybee on the door and usually I try to kill a bee before it stings me. This particular morning, I just could not do that. I'd been looking at Jesus for an hour. I didn't feel like killing anything, not even a bee.

The love of Jesus is the only kind of love that will overcome the negativity of the world. If we would just spend an hour looking into the face of Jesus, we can be changed.

I went over to that little bee and I just picked it up in my hand and it took it to the door and gently let it go. As I did, I said to it, "Here is your freedom little bee, you have done no harm to me. Take your wings and fly today to your loved ones far away. Fly on wings of love and know, out of love I let you go. You are as dear to me as you are to Mrs. Bee."

The love of Jesus is redemptive. It can make a person who wants to kill something (like a little bee) and want the bee be free. The love of Jesus is the only kind of love that will overcome the negativity of the world. If we would just spend an hour looking into the face of Jesus, we can be changed. When I looked at Jesus for an hour, He overcame the urge to hurt in me and I know there is an urge to hurt in me. If it weren't for Jesus Christ, I probably would have really hurt somebody. I probably wouldn't have meant to do it, but I would have. I know that and so I need access to God's love, which I experience in Jesus.

For many of us, when we take our devotional time, instead of communing with God by reading God's Word, the Bible, we read a devotional book written by someone else to get an idea about what God thinks. We don't need to do this. How would you like it if you wanted to talk with your lover but instead he would sit and read a book about you that somebody else wrote? It's an insult to God when we can't even sit down in His presence and look at Him, and read his words from scripture. Prayer is just giving God and the Holy Spirit your complete and total attention.

I was returning from a one day Ashram in Anderson, Indiana and on my way home, I had the most amazing experience. It was almost like meeting Jesus on the Emmaus Road. It was close to Mother's Day and I was one of the happiest persons who ever lived. My heart was just singing the praises of the Lord.

I had just received the most wonderful letter from my son. He's 20 years old and in the Air Force and he wrote, "Mother, you're going to get this before Mother's Day because I want it to be there on time. You know, I've been sitting here in the barracks thinking of all the things that I know about you as a person and I was trying to think of the one thing that stands out as most important. Mother, I want to say, that the most important thing that I can remember about you is this: You put my feet upon the Jesus way of life."

I tell you when I got that card, everything within me cried out, "Oh, God, wouldn't it be wonderful if every mother's son would say that to her on Mother's Day." That's the only thing any mother wants to hear her son say. You don't want to be told you're beautiful. You don't want to be told you're a good cook, but if your children come to you and thank you for the one thing that means more to them than life itself... that you helped them to find the Jesus way of life. This flood of love came over me and as I was driving along.

However, at exactly 8:30 that same morning suddenly my heart began to break. I cried and cried and cried like I had never cried before. I couldn't stop it. I was crying so hard, I thought I was going to have to pull off the road. Then I began to have real pain in my heart just like a million little knives stabbing me. I thought I was having a heart attack. But the Lord said, "Keep driving."

Then the Lord began to talk to me about sin and told me to think of all the sin that I could conceive of and multiply it by a million and then I would have some idea of the power of Satan's hold on people. God said, "Mary, you don't even know what sin is. You only know how to spell it. You don't know what it really is. You haven't even thought of some of the sin that occurs in this world." As I thought of all the sin in the world, all the evil of this sin of the world, God told me that on the cross, every bit of that was run straight through Jesus' heart. Just think of it and so I wept some more as if I would never stop crying.

However, at exactly 9:00 am, just 30 minutes later, my crying stopped. God flipped the switch and showed me what the love of God is like. He said, "Mary, one drop of my love is more potent than all the sin in the world." Just think of that. Why we can't even conceive of what grace is and what love is when God offers it. So often I have marveled at the fact that Jesus died on the cross for me. However, I've only seen half of the cross when I look at it from man's side. Now I was seeing the cross from God's perspective.

I know human beings can sacrifice their lives for someone else. I've seen it. If your child were drowning, I know there isn't a person in this room who wouldn't risk his or her life to save that drowning child. We would all do that. You can suffer for others. You might even learn to forgive others. You might lay down your life and recall what Jesus said, "Greater love hath no man than this, that he would lay down his life for his friend."

So we can lay down our lives for our friends. That's as high as man can go, but when I look at what God did on Calvary...that is another story. If I had a son like Jesus and I were God and I saw these wicked, wicked people nailing Him to that cross, scourging Him, spitting on Him, and running thorns into His flesh, I'm afraid would have done something to them. I would surely do something to stop it, but just think about the depth of God's love for us to let that happen to His own Son and not do one single thing to us, we who have caused his son such pain. That's real love, that's God's love, that's divine love.

God's love allows you to kill Him and He goes right on loving you. When you run a sword into Jesus, the very blood that comes out of the wound is what heals you and makes you well. That's the kind of love that God wants us to demonstrate to others. However, I know that I don't have it.

One time a woman came to talk with me about a problem. She told me that her husband was an alcoholic. With kindness I said to her, "My dear girl, I hate to discourage you and disillusion you but your alcoholic husband is not your problem. Your problem is yourself. Nobody is anybody else's problem. Our problem is our own un-surrendered self. I continued, "You are looking at your husband and his faults and you say he's your problem but he isn't. Your pride is your problem."

She didn't like my comment. But I continued, "Now if I want to help you, I might have to hurt you but if I hurt you and you

> God's love allows you to kill Him and He goes right on loving you. When you run a sword into Jesus, the very blood that comes out of the wound is what heals you and makes you well. That's the kind of love that God wants us to demonstrate to others.

get well, it'll be a blessing. I don't care whether you like me or not, but I do care if you love Jesus. I know if you love Jesus, you can go home and love your husband as unto the Lord. Let's analyze the situation. How do you react when your husband comes home drunk?" She said, "I don't want anything to do with him." I continued, "You told God that you would love Him for better or for worse. Didn't you mean it when you said that? You think your husband is being unfaithful to you, well, you've been unfaithful to him."

The moment you stop believing in a person, you're unfaithful to that person. I told her, "You know something? Your pride makes your resent the way he acts. You think you should have a better deal coming. I'll tell you something, "You ought to spend the whole winter shoveling your own sidewalks, paying your own bills...that and the whole shooting match and you'd be glad to have a little help." I continued, "You know something, I'll guarantee that you could really love that man but your pride's involved. You don't think he should treat you this way. All right, maybe you shouldn't treat him that way."

I added, "Now you can't overcome this impasse by yourself, but the Spirit of Jesus Christ in you can make you love your husband as unto the Lord. So get off his back and get on his team. That might help him." "Has your ridicule and your sarcasm and your throwing him out of the house ... has that changed him any?" She responded, "No, it's made him worse." I responded, "Why don't you try the Jesus way? What have you got to lose? You can always get a divorce if it doesn't work, but go home and try the Jesus Way first, before you say you've tried everything."

I continued, "You can't do it, honey, until you surrender yourself and your pride to Jesus. Jesus is the only One who can help you love your husband the way he needs to be loved. He's the only one that can hold you in check, so Jesus can help your husband." She knelt down, surrendered herself and her pride to Jesus and she prayed that Jesus Christ could love her husband and help her to love him as unto Jesus.

She said to me when she started to leave, "You know, Mary, I'd give anything if my husband would come to the church tonight. I think you could help him." I said, "No, I couldn't. I can't even help myself, and don't you dare go home and start to reform him. You go home and love him as unto the Lord and leave him to Jesus. Jesus will transform him, but you leave him alone. He's God's problem now. You go home and love him."

Don't you dare go home and start to reform him. You go home and love him as unto the Lord and leave him to Jesus. Jesus will transform him, but you leave him alone. He's God's problem now. You go home and love him."

I continued, "You know something, I told God once about a situation where everything in it was unchristian and unjust and I was complaining to God about it, as if He didn't know." God said, "You're right, Mary, there is something very unchristian about this whole deal and it's your attitude toward it." I said, "God's never been on my side. Every time I take a problem about somebody else to Him, I'm always wrong and God never agrees with me. Remember that. Don't look at your husband's problem. Look at him and love him as unto the Lord."

She went home that afternoon and when we had the evening altar service, a great big six foot two man came down the aisle at the end of the meeting with tears streaming down his face and another fellow with him and this little woman in between them. I said to him, "What's happened to you?" He answered, "If anybody had told me at three o'clock this afternoon that I'd be in a church at an altar, I'd have thought they were crazy. At three o'clock this afternoon, I was in a tavern with my buddy. This is my drinking buddy, we drink together all the time. We've got wives just alike. You'd think they were twin sisters. Nag, nag, nag, nag, nothing suits them, no matter how much money we bring in, it's never enough, they've got to have more. They don't want us, they want what we've got but they don't love us." He continued, "My wife told me today that if I didn't stop drinking, she'd leave me and I thought, 'Boy, if that will get rid of her, I'll go out and really get drunk, so I went to the tavern."

"I was there until three o'clock this afternoon. We brought a case of beer home. We were really going to have a party to show her that I'm boss in my house." He continued, "As I came in the door, I staggered and spilled some of the beer cans on the floor and one rolled over by where she was standing. I ducked when she picked it up. I knew she'd throw it at me and instead of that, she put it on the table and she came over to me with love in her eyes, and said, 'You didn't hurt yourself, did you?'"

"I looked at her face and I was almost all sober. I thought to myself, that's not the old witch I was fighting with this morning, what's happened to her?" He continued, "As I looked into her eyes, I didn't see the disgust that I am so used to seeing. I just saw love, she even treated my friend as if he were a human being instead of a dog. She had never let him in the house before. She only lets the dog in, she never lets my friend in. It's my house, I paid for it and he can't even come in the house, but today she asked him in. She made us each a cup of coffee. We just sat there and looked at each other."

"We couldn't even speak and we certainly didn't drink any beer. Then she went in the bedroom and she came back out and she said she was going to church. She told me that she had run into you this afternoon and you were a Christian and she thought that you would tell her that she ought to get a divorce and leave me and that she deserved a better husband. However, you told her she'd better get on her knees and ask Jesus Christ to help her to deserve the one she had, that she didn't even know how to love me as unto the Lord and that's why I was drinking excessively."

The man continued, "When she told me she was going to church to get another lesson from Jesus on how to love me, I thought, 'Brother, I've got to go with her or she might not get it all. I knew that the church was made up of sinners and I ..." I mean, "of saints, and I knew I'd be uncomfortable in their presence so I asked my buddy to come with me because at least I'd feel comfortable with him. We sat at the very back of the church expecting that you and everyone else would be down on this and down on that and we did not want to be too close to all of those judgments."

He said, "You know, you came up on my blindside because you said that you were in the gutter when Jesus Christ found you and He took you up like a little orphaned baby and held you to His breast and loved you and my soul cried out, 'Oh, Jesus, love me that way. I don't want to be an alcoholic, but I can't help it.'" He continued, "I kind of wanted to come to that prayer altar but I was too ashamed to come, because all of the lights were on and everybody might look at me." "You know, young lady, you must be psychic because you asked for ushers to turn the lights down and I wanted to go to the altar but wanted to sneak away from my buddy because I thought if I didn't find anything at the altar, I didn't want him to make fun of me, so I tried to slip away without his seeing me but he pulled on my coattail and said, 'Wait a minute, I want to go with you.'"

"We came down to this altar of prayer like a couple of school boys and the minute my knees hit that altar, I met Jesus Christ in a very real way." Amen, Lord. "I don't think I'll ever want to drink again because I've found Jesus and I don't need alcohol anymore." "With Jesus Christ and this little woman, how can I lose?" She was looking at that guy as if he owned the moon. "Boy, I'm telling you, if somebody looks at you like that, you don't want to get drunk."

Some people are alcoholics because somebody who didn't really love Jesus looked at them with disgust instead of love. I tell you, I've never seen a person saved when somebody stood over them with a philosophy and said, "You ought to be as good as me."

However, when you get down on your knees beside them and say, "I'm no different than you are, except I met Jesus and He has healed me and made me well," folks will ask, "Who is your Physician? Let me know His name," and so this love of God has got to be in us. It's got to be the Word become Flesh in us, if this unsaved world is ever going to want anything that we have to offer.

Let me tell you another related story. Christians are supposed to care and they are supposed to be understanding. I went to a Christian Ashram one time and a woman came up to me who we learned later had just been released from a psychiatric institution. Her name was Helen. She had heard that Christians were people who cared and that they loved other people, and sought to understand them.

The weather was hot in Texas and everyone's tempers were short and Helen asked the Ashram manager to change her room 13 times in an hour and a half because none of the rooms were cool enough for her. None of the rooms suited her and so he said to her, "I don't think you're going to like any of our rooms. I think you'd better go home. You might like your own room better." That girl knew immediately that her assumption that Christians are supposed to care was incorrect. She had just learned that the Ashram manager did not care. She thought to herself that Christians were no different than anybody else. She experienced that lack of caring everywhere, in the institution, at home...everywhere. She started to pack her suitcase but one little Christian girl, went to Helen and said, "Please don't go home. Please don't go home. Give us another chance."

That little girl came to me and said, "Mary, please talk to this woman. Please don't let her go home in utter defeat." I said, "I'll talk to her. I don't know that I can help her any," but when Helen came in and sat down, she started to talk to me. She looked at me and said, "I don't think you're religious. I think you're nuts." I said, "I am nuts, but I'm happy and you're not. Look, you want to find out how I got this way? I don't care what you think of me but I know somebody who really loves you and I want you to know that. He healed me, He can heal you."

Helen's face began to twitch and I was worried that she might have a collapse. She started to cry, crying like her heart would break. I don't know anything about counseling but I know one thing, when a person is so emotionally upset and they've been crying for a long time as if their heart would break, you don't tell them to stop, dry their eyes, have a prayer, and come eat their supper. You just don't tell people that, if you love them. My heart was just breaking for this girl, because I've been like that girl, but Jesus saved me in time and I remembered that.

I felt that I did not have sufficient spiritual power to help her to find what she needed. I wasn't a bridge enough. There wasn't enough of me to bridge the gap between Jesus and her and so I started to cry. She then put her arms around me and said, "Why are you crying?" I responded, "I don't know except that one night I looked into the eyes of Jesus and He healed me and I don't seem to have the ability to help you see Jesus. I sure lack something but Jesus doesn't."

I continued, "I know that if you'd go to the altar and give your life to Him, like I did when my life was bankrupt, I know He will heal you because He healed me." That comment seemed to do it. She then said, "Do you mean to tell me that you were emotionally unstable like this?" I said, "Oh, I was, but Jesus changed everything for me." She said, "Mary, I really want what you have. How do I get it?" I responded, "You don't have to get it, honey. All you have to do is to take it, just take it. Kneel down here, accept Jesus Christ, and turn your life over to Him. Let Him worry about you and you'll be happy."

That girl did it. When I got home, a month later, she wrote me a letter. She said her husband, a wealthy man, was so happy that she came back to him well, happy and radiant. He was so indebted to Jesus Christ that he offered to give his wife a maid to work in her house eight hours a day so that she could offer full time Christian service. He added, "Don't take any money for your Christian service. Just do it out of gratitude to Jesus for what He has done for you. He has restored your mind, your soul, and your body. We owe Him everything. Go out and do it for somebody else, honey, to keep your healing going."

Her letter continued, "Mary, I prayed about it and Jesus said the one place on earth He really needed me was in a home for developmentally disabled children, because adults are never patient with these children. They need more love and more care than other children and because I know that Christians care, I wanted to be with them. So I went to that home and worked eight hours a day with these little children and every day I tell them that Jesus is proud of them, that Jesus loves them." She said, "My life is fulfilled. I've got a channel to throw this blessing back into the world that Jesus gave me when He healed me."

A year ago, when I was in Texas, a girl came up to me and she said, "Have you heard about Helen? Her body is riddled with cancer," and I said, "Uh-oh, I'll bet her faith will be challenged now." I called her on the telephone and I said, "Helen, they tell me that you have cancer." She says, "Oh, yes, I've got cancer, but don't forget I've got Jesus, too, and cancer's not so bad if you've got Jesus. But, oh, mental illness without Him is just hell on earth. I'd rather have cancer and Jesus any day than to be mentally ill without Him."

My friends, Christians care, but Helen's soul would have hung in a balance if God hadn't had that sympathetic little girl who didn't know theology, but she knew human need when she saw it.

Last Holy Week, I spent about five hours early in the morning, from one am until the very early morning hours just looking … just looking at Jesus. I was trying to relive His life in my mind. I sat there and I thought of what this song says, "Lead me to Calvary. Let me really look at Him on the cross. Let me really see what God's love is … at the foot of Calvary."

As I went through those hours and the suffering and torture that Jesus experienced, this little poem came to me."You knew the cold Gethsemane. You suffered pain and agony. You bled and died on Calvary, for love of me, for love of me, but when I saw what love would do and saw all my sin had put You through, I saw the cross, the cup and knew, I, too, would die for love of You."

Shall we pray?

Our Father, tonight, we pray that the Holy Spirit, who is the love of God in the hearts of us will come into us and bring this love of God that makes us Christians who care. Tenderize our hearts, Lord. Make us so soft that the simplest cry of a derelict would touch us. Oh, God, help us to see tonight that if the world is in hell, in part that is because there are not enough Christians who care enough to leave their television sets to go out and share the love of Christ with others. Now take our hand and put it into His and everything that we have and follow Him this day. May this be a day of Thy Presence. We ask Your blessing upon us and may the Holy Spirit enlighten us, and fill us with the glory of Jesus. We ask it in His name, Amen.

E. Stanley Jones, Mary Webster and others in Japan

THE INFLUENCE

OF

MARY WEBSTER

E. STANLEY JONES

EDITOR'S NOTE

To my knowledge this sermon is the only one that E. Stanley Jones preached about a specific person. Jones was convinced that the laity are the most powerful conveyors of the message of Jesus Christ and would repeatedly affirm their significance to the Christian Church. Jones was surely delighted to discover a laywoman with such a powerful message about the transforming power of Jesus Christ and with such gifts to share it with others.

The reader may find familiar material in this sermon, but rather than remove any redundancies or previously shared illustrations the editor has elected to keep it "whole cloth."

MY TALK WILL BE a little different tonight as I want to talk about a person who lives among us now and who illustrates some wonderful aspects of a life fully surrendered to Jesus Christ. I do this with some hesitation knowing how difficult it is to "evaluate" a person while they're alive but whatever happens in the future, I can say that the life that has influenced me the most this year was of a woman who grew up and still lives on a farm.

As I look back across the years I find certain people influence me at certain periods. At one period of time, it was Booker T. Washington, At another it was Gandhi. Though not a Christian, he pointed me to the Christian gospel again and again, especially to the cross. However, as I consider this last year, I find that the woman I will describe to you has led me deeper into the life of Christ than anyone else during this year and so I want to share with you some of the things that she has taught me.

I know that she'd be the last person on earth to want to be talked about. I said to her some time ago, I said, "Mary, I hope that this attention and praise that is coming to you will have you fall to your knees and not go to your head." She looked back and she said, "But Brother

Stanley, honestly your comment didn't touch me, didn't have my name on it, because I know it has little or no reference to me," and I believe that she meant that. I'm sharing this example of Mary tonight because a great many people think that you have to have special endowment or special privileges to walk into the kingdom of God and take its resources. I offer this illustration because it shows that the latchstring of the kingdom of God is available to everyone.

> ... many people think that you have to have special endowment or special privileges to walk into the kingdom of God and take its resources. I offer this illustration because it shows that the latchstring of the kingdom of God is available to everyone.

The first time I saw Mary Webster was in a meeting in Peoria, Illinois. She sat in the second row of the church with a little boy. She was eager-faced and looked very young, but was the mother of two children. She appeared so eager and I remember noticing her as I came in, but thought little about it. She told me afterwards that she came to hear me speak on India. Instead, she heard me speak on God and she found Him that evening. I admit I had nothing to do with her conversion. It was immediate and direct apparently from the Spirit of God.

She's progressed further in these two and a half years since she's been a Christian, gone further than anybody I've ever seen go in a lifetime, and I say that advisedly. I thought that perhaps I was mistaken, but two of my friends, one of whom is here, Brother John Bigeleisen and the other Kathleen Bailey, both of them agreed with me that she has perhaps the most remarkable spiritual character that they've come in contact with. Kathleen Bailey said, "She is, I think the most remarkable spiritual character in the world." That may be an overestimation, but here's an ordinary woman, who walked into the kingdom of God and took it over by hand full, arms full, and in great simplicity has demonstrated the power of the kingdom of God.

Brother John is here tonight, and you'll forgive me if I tell this story, but the story goes that when brother John saw Mary two years ago at the Kerrville, Texas Ashram, and talked with her, he came into his room afterwards and began to dance. You can hardly imagine Brother John undertaking a dance, but he said, "For the first time in my life, I've seen a child of the kingdom of God." Somebody in that Ashram said that she looks as though she's swallowed an electric light bulb, and she does. She's radiant. Let me share some aspects of Mary that tell you of her spirit.

Very early in her spiritual journey, Mary came to the Kerrville Ashram and became friendly with one of the African American women and said to her, "I'd like to go back with you on the bus." The African American friend said, "But you know the segregation on the buses in Texas." Mary continued, "But I'm going with you."

Writing about this experience, Mary said, "I've learned some things from having to bring in the cows with the bull from the pasture," she said, "I've found out that the thing to do is to let them know who's boss, look them straight in the eye and let them know who's boss, so I determined that I was going to look the bus driver straight in the eye, if he said anything, I would say to him, 'I've got red blood in my veins just like hers, and I belong to a kingdom higher than the great state of Texas, the kingdom of God, and it's color blind.'" As a result, the driver got in the bus and looked back at Mary sitting next to her friend in the segregated section of the bus and sort of grinned and sat down and drove the bus. Mary's African American friend turned to her and said, "Thank God honey for the real thing that you get at the Ashram," and Mary replied, "If I had more of the real thing I would explode."

She's simplicity itself. She exteriorizes her thinking. She was in a meeting some time ago and the minister was a liberal modernist, and he said, "Jesus is dead. They buried him, he's dead." Sister Mary sitting halfway back in the congregation and forgetting where she was blurted out, "Oh no you're wrong. He's alive. I was talking with Him this morning."

Mary has great insights. When you sit and listen to her, she pours out a flood of spiritual insights that makes you sit back and say, "Well, where did those insights come from? Where did she get them?" I received a letter from Mary today and she told how she and Sister Kathleen Bailey were seated in their room talking and Mary said, "You know, when I get started with my enthusiasms about Jesus, I forget everything. I was pouring it out and when I finished I turned around and there was Kathleen's husband, a doctor, seated on the other side of the room, listening, spellbound at what Mary was saying, and she said, "I didn't know he was there, but he certainly got an earful."

251

Mary is open and frank. She walked down an aisle of a train one day and on an impulse stopped at a man said, "You've got a Christian face. You look like a Christian. Are you one?" The man said, "Well, I'm a minister," and they sat down had a wonderful time. She has insights. Here is an example, "At the end of every high expectation there is the inevitable bucket of cold water." And another, "There's two ways to meet that cold water, one dodging and then you get wet and feel sorry for yourself, and full of self-pity." She continued, "The other way to meet it is head-on, the way you take a shower. Walk straight into it with expectancy and then step out of it refreshed."

Her whole philosophy of life is that simple and that straightforward. There really are two ways to meet life, one dodging life and the other is with expectation and walking right into it and walking out the other side — refreshed. I said to Mary some time ago, "Sister Mary, I'm gathering material for a new book *How to Grow Spiritually.*"I continued, "Have you got any ideas or materials? If so, send them along." She wrote back and said, "Brother Stanley I have a suggestion to make. If you've got any new ideas you send them along to me and I'll put them in practice to see whether they'll work or not. I'd be your guinea pig."

I'll read at random now several extracts from her powerful letters, "Lately I've had a tremendous experience with the Lord. How I wish you were here in person that I might share it with you. You would understand it. Brother Stanley, it is so marvelous to me that I can scarcely tell it all to anyone. Sometimes it would be kind of you if you would let me share all the glory with you. Jesus amazes me with all that he gives me and does to me and with me.

It's like a fairy tale come true. I'm like the pumpkin that he touched with his wand and turned into a lovely carriage."

Here is another, "You probably have heard the story of the child who had a fan and she showed it to a famous painter who said, 'Let me have your fan and I'll paint a beautiful picture on it." The child grabbed hold of the fan and said, "Give me the fan back. It's mine. I'm not going to let you spoil it.' How often do we tell God, 'This is my life. You might spoil it if I let you paint something on it'? But oh the unspeakable joy and glory that comes when we learn to say, 'Here Lord, use me.' Brother Stanley I'm so happy right now I could shout. Every day is that way, just filled with joy and gladness."

A couple of years after Mary came to the Lord, she had a terrible car accident in which her husband was killed and her two boys were badly hurt as was Mary and her sister in law, May. This letter was written to me just after her sister-in-law came out from an 8-month stay in the hospital following the accident. "My blessed sister-

> She's simplicity itself. She exteriorizes her thinking. She was in a meeting some time ago and the minister was a liberal modernist, and he said, "Jesus is dead. They buried him, he's dead." Sister Mary sitting halfway back in the congregation and forgetting where she was blurted out, "Oh no you're wrong. He's alive. I was talking with Him this morning."

in-law, May, is home at last, she will never be fully well again but she can walk on crutches some, though it's quite an effort. The Lord has granted to me the privilege of caring for her now at the time that she needs it. He always blesses me with good things."

Mary continues, "I make a good little nurse and it will be such fun. We're just getting along fine, the children, May and I. We're so grateful for being together again. My sister-in-law is 70. She loves being home again and the children and I are so happy that we're all together again. The children are very loving to her. Really the Lord ought to make me pay for the privilege of living with her. She's staging a real comeback at 70 years of age. Our friends call us Ruth and Naomi. The doctors said May would never walk but she is walking and her spirit hasn't been broken. Praise God. I told you what I told the carpenter who said I was a fool to tie myself down taking care of this sister-in-law. I said, 'I'm not tied down, I'm cemented here with the love of Christ in my heart.'"

Mary looks on everything and does everything for the love of God. However, one day she said, that there were certain things about tending to her sister-in-law's physical needs that she didn't like. Mary explained, "But Jesus came to me and said, 'Mary I know you don't like to do these things very much, but I do. I want to do them for her but I can't and I have no one to do it for me, except you. Will you do it for me?'" She then said, "Now I care for May for the love of Christ. Everything I find myself doing is for the love of Christ."

After she was converted Mary said that her chickens began to lay far more eggs than they had ever laid before and that they were bigger. Her friends wanted to understand how this was happening. She said, "It's no secret. I love these hens and I gather them around me and thank them for their cooperation, and they gather around me and they seem to love laying eggs and I love them."

Here's an extract from another letter, "On Sunday March the 16th, I was asked to speak in a church 65 miles from here on the topic, now don't laugh, Pentecost. The flu's been very prevalent here lately and the morning that I was to speak I did not feel well at all.   I still felt badly as I was driving to the church and thought that I would need to turn around and go home to bed. Then I remembered what you did at your meeting in Vellore (India) and so I too prayed the same prayer you taught me, changing on the first letter of the word rain to P for pain."

I had previously told her about a time in India where we were having a final meeting of an evangelistic series at Vellore. The meeting was out in the open courtyard of the college, a couple thousand people were there, and we wanted to make that night the special night for new decisions for Christ among this mostly non-Christian audience. When I began to speak it began to rain. It seldom rains in Vellore that time of the year but it began to rain, and I said, "Oh God these people certainly do need rain, but please can you hold it off until we get through with this meeting?" and the rain stopped, and we continued with the meeting where several hundred people made decisions for Christ.

I had told Mary about this experience and so she adapted my prayer and prayed, 'Oh father I deserve this pain, but please hold it up until this meeting is over. I want to serve you today but I'm not well enough trained to preach with so much pain. I'd be happy to accept it tomorrow. In any case thy grace is sufficient for me.' And the pain went away.

Here is another excerpt from a letter, "Brother Stanley when I was Chicago speaking, a peculiar thing happened, I was trying to impress upon the hearers the importance of surrendering to Christ now, as each moment might be the last, and all of a sudden out of my mouth came this inspiration. The spiritual message of Noah and the ark is don't wait until the flood comes to build your boat. Build it while the weather is fair and when the flood does come, you have but to step inside your ark of faith and ride on top of the flood. I know you may be laughing at my illustration but it just came to me and I said it and I think that it made them think about being prepared for trouble because trouble does come. It's a little too late to think clearly when the mind is flooded with trouble and when that happens, we usually flounder."

Here's another one. "For quite some time now, I've noticed that everyone I meet, even if it is for the first time, calls me by my first name. Recently I met the superintendent of the public school systems of Kewanee, Illinois and he asked me if I would come into his office and see him when I had a free moment. He's a very austere person and very formal with those he works with daily. In spite of his demeanor and formality, he called me Mary the whole time. He met with me for two hours and spent the whole time discussing religion. He's very intellectually-focused and kept asking me over and over again, 'How?' I told him "how" I met Christ and what has happened to me since then. I told him how simple and wonderful life had become for me and how the knowledge of Christ's presence held me safe and sure regardless of circumstances." I was very eager that he surrender his life to Christ.

"I tried every way I knew to get that pill of complete surrender down his throat (not literally of course) and I found that surrender is one pill that isn't sugarcoated. It's just plain bitter no matter how you take it. The man listened but of course only he and God knows if he swallowed the "surrender" pill or not. It's rather difficult for me to make myself understood for even when I was using the plainest language; he kept telling me to speak more concretely. I thought that I was. It struck me that he was trying to come to Christ through reason instead of surrender, but of course I could be wrong.

Mary continued, "He impressed me as a rather lonely man because when I

"At the end of every high expectation there is the inevitable bucket of cold water." "There's two ways to meet that cold water, one dodging and then you get wet and feel sorry for yourself, and full of self-pity." "The other way to meet it is head-on, the way you take a shower. Walk straight into it with expectancy and then step out of it refreshed."

spoke about Christ's presence giving me inner assurance and release from hurt, his face lit up as if some chord of recognition was struck. This man was so close to his surrender to Christ, but close doesn't count. He said he'd like to feel on the inside the way my face looked on the outside. He wants joy, of course that's what the whole

257

world wants, but only Christ within us can produce real joy. It all seems so simple and yet it is very hard to offer surrender to others. They get to the point of surrender and then they try taking me down a side street, instead of going one step more to the way."

Here is another bit from a letter, "When I was talking to Jesus tonight He told me that He was going to Help me to grow inwardly. He said the most important thing is to always remember to keep my eyes on Him and listen to Him when things get tough. He said He wants me to learn to be patient when it is difficult to be patient, to be cheerful and happy even when others are sour and grouchy. He wants me to learn to stop when He says, 'That's enough,' and to go when He says, 'The road is clear.' He wants me to learn to keep still when I feel like talking and to speak when He tells me to speak and say what He wants me to say, even if I don't want to. He wants me to see that when I am called upon to do something that I have an opportunity to grow and that it is for Him that I labor, and not for the world. He said He would never call me to do anything without being given His power to do what He requested."

Here is another interesting Mary story, and here I quote Mary. "The other day I was talking with a girl who lost her mother a year ago and she asked me if I didn't feel sad, afraid and lonely just as she was currently experiencing. After she left, I wrote down the words that came into my heart when she asked me that question.

Sad, afraid, lonely.
I am not sad.
I know the joy of a heart's full surrender.

I'm living in splendor.
I'm not sad, I'm not afraid.
He sends His grace in abundance to bless me.
I feel him caress me.
I'm not afraid.
I'm not alone, I have God's love and
His spirit to guide me.
He is walking beside me.
I'm not alone."

She's been able to impact her two children with her spirit. One son, Teddy, is 10, another Claude is five. Teddy went to the Kerrville Ashram this last week and on the drive to the Ashram he told me that he was raising 10 pigs and said, "Brother Stanley, I'm going to give one of those pigs to India," without my asking. Later the little boy told me that he often goes out to teach one of the hens the 23rd Psalm, and when she clucks he says, "Now she's getting it."

And here is another Mary story, "Teddy and Claude were upstairs in their bedroom a while back and I overheard Teddy telling Claude that he must be kind to a little boy in school who had no mother to get him ready for school and see that he was clean and that because Claude did have a mother, he should be very kind to the other child. Some of the children had been picking on the little boy and making fun of him and were not playing with him because he was not as clean as the others. At the close of this little brotherly "lecture" to Claude, Teddy said to him, "And besides, Claude, you can't act the way the other children do because you're a Christian." I was so glad to hear that conversation and so I went into their room and hugged them both. That is what the Ashram does for a little boy of 10."

Another excerpt from a Mary letter: "Nothing anyone says to me can insult me or hurt my feelings anymore, for there's nothing anyone can say to me that I haven't already said to myself." That's a good way to head off insults. Just say worse things to yourself so nothing that anybody else can say is as bad as what you have already said to yourself." I often have done the same thing. When I look at myself in a mirror I say, "Stanley Jones, you're an ass," and I really mean it, so when somebody else says it I say, "That's all right. I've already heard that."

Mary once said, nothing anyone says can flatter me anymore because no matter what anyone says, there's always the picture in my mind of what I was before Christ, while all others are now seeing just what happened to me after Christ. When God has a message to give to the world He uses the first available instrument He finds, regardless of its capacities or deficits. I found a good picture of myself in God's hands while reading Matthew 12:20, "The bruised reed, will it not break, and the smoking flax, will it not be quenched?" Jesus wants a pen to write with but I'm just a bruised and broken bit of reed. Well, He'll use me until something better comes along. He wants a light but I'm just a dim-lit burning wick, but still He'll use me inferior as I am."

To show another element of the character of her Christianity, let me return to the car accident that I told you about earlier. When the accident took place she was entitled to $18,000 as compensation from the truck driver who caused the accident, but her lawyer said, "I can get more money for you by pursuing another legal angle in this care. I can get you $25,000." Mary said, "But, the driver wasn't morally responsible for the accident. It might be legal but it won't be moral to do that. No, I couldn't take the extra $7,000." She refused to solicit the additional money although she had a legal right to do so. At the close her lawyer took her up to meet the judge and he said, "My dear, I'm glad to shake the hand of a real Christian." She responded to the judge, "I do not want to tell you about the Mary before Christ, as it isn't nice to talk about people after they're dead."

I told him "how" I met Christ and what has happened to me since then. I told him how simple and wonderful life had become for me and how the knowledge of Christ's presence held me safe and sure regardless of circumstances."

She once wrote to me, "Brother Stanley in the name of Jesus, please expect bigger things of me, and help me to surpass your expectations. I'm not asking for flattery. I'm begging you to take me out to that point of no return, out of the safety zone where nothing is predictable. There are big things to be done in this world that won't wait forever so that's why I ask you to dream up the greatest possible thing you can think of that a woman can do and share your dream with me, and then hand me the pick and shovel and tell me to go to work." Wouldn't you pastors like that, if your church members would make that kind of offer to you.

Mary continues, "Before my conversion I was trying to live in spite of, but after reading your book, "The Way *to Power and Poise,"* the very power you wrote about began to change the words "in spite of," to "because of" and everything within me began to mellow. My attitude before Christ came within me was that of defiance. 'I don't care what you do to me, life. I'm determined to live in spite of anything you can do to stop me,' but after reading *The Way to Power and Poise,* you took me to where the aviators call the point of no return. I didn't have enough fuel left in my tank to go back to where I started and couldn't just stay suspended in mid-air, so out of sheer necessity I had to go on to Christ."

And I said to Mary, "But you see what you did? You 'depth charged' your own depths. Christ brought you back to life, alive and you looked life straight in the face and said, 'Dear precious life, I had you all wrong. I will no longer tolerate you. I accept you all in all just as you come.' Now life and you are no longer at swords points with one another. You are friends, and the more you invest in life, the greater dividends you will draw." Mary has life with a capital L. Mary added, "I will accept life just as it comes, because of Jesus," and you will see what that means when in a few minutes I read you her final letter.

Mary further wrote, "I've been studying the subject of humility; God finds me a very difficult student for I just don't understand the word "humility" in all its fullness. God told me to find each day something to do that is beneath me or that I feel is beneath me. However, I just can't seem to find anything that is beneath me. What can it be? I'm almost certain I shall remain in the first grade until I learn this supreme lesson. Can you help me?"

"You see Brother Stanley, when you let me take your prayer hour each evening at the Green Lake Ashram, you really provided me with a wonderful spiritual education, for it was there that I received, you might say, a divine imperative from two passages of scripture. The first was Revelation 11:1, 'where I was given a measuring reed like a staff.' That was as far as the spirit would let me read that night. However I could not stop thinking about that passage of scripture, especially the word "reed." I wanted to know what the word *reed* meant in this context and so I went to a dictionary and looked up the meaning."

Mary is the only person that I know who will stop you when you are talking and ask, "What does that word mean?" Then she'll note it down. Mary has no inhibitions about asking you the meaning of a word. She writes down what the pastors are saying and looks up any word she does not understand. She discovered that the word reed was defined as a 'A pastoral pipe, a mouth tube of a musical instrument.'" Mary meditated the rest of the hour on that meaning. It seemed to say to her that God has given to her a mouth tube, a voice, through which can flow music because the tube is open at both ends, and He's given it to her for a purpose to develop it for His service.

Mary continues, "The next evening, I deliberately opened the Bible to Matthew to read something, I hoped to find something quite different from the Revelation passage and I had a sense that God had a message for me and wanted to deliver it. However, I was not sure that I wanted the message. Well, I was reading about Peter's denial of Jesus and in Matthew 26:72 my eyes fell on the words, 'For thy speech betrayeth thee.' I nearly dropped the book. From Omega back to Alpha, this time I knew God was trying to give me a message.

"So the next afternoon I cornered dear Brother Mark and said to him, 'Brother Mark, everyone up here is very anxious to point out our good points, but no one will be honest with me and tell me what is wrong with how I speak so that I may correct it. However, I know that you are honest and I believe what you say and because I know you like me, will you be honest enough and kind enough to point out the weaknesses with my speech so that I may grow?'" There are not many people who are going around and asking, "Now tell me what's wrong with me so I can grow." Most of us are dodging that sort of question.

Mary continues, "You should have seen the look on his face. It was precious. He wanted to say something to me, but he was afraid of offending me so I told him he would do me a favor, and so bless his heart he said, 'Well, if you would suffer a suggestion, it is your voice. It has a tenseness in it that isn't in your character. It is too high and if you would try pitching it lower and speaking more slowly, you would be easy to listen to.' The poor man looked as if he had done one of the hardest things he'd been called upon to do for the Lord."

"As you know Brother Stanley, I never admired anyone more than I did him at that moment, for it takes a lot of courage and deep compassion for a person to risk disfavor by telling them something that might offend them and make them like you less. I told him I knew he must like me a lot to be willing to help me and I wouldn't tell anyone about our discussion and we would never mention it again, but if when we saw each other the next time and if I had made any improvement we would laugh and rejoice over it together."

"I went to work on it my voice right away and bought a book entitled *So to Speak,* which is excellent and presented me with helpful challenges. The book described how to walk to make breathing easier, and how to form words, how to listen to your own voice and criticize it constructively. Really, I've never had so much fun and done so much hard work in my life. I recently received an invitation to speak in a church in Chicago, with Brother Philip and Sister Anna and several other Ashramites, and Sister Anna said she noticed some improvement in my voice, and someone else said they also noticed some improvements. Oh, I thought, this is really fun. Maybe God can make me a good speaker for his Kingdom yet. I believe in miracles. In fact I live on them."

When I was talking to Jesus tonight He told me that He was going to Help me to grow inwardly. He said the most important thing is to always remember to keep my eyes on Him and listen to Him when things get tough.

"Another incident about that Sunday. It was a Black church on the south side of Chicago that had invited me to come. I was very much looking forward to speaking in a Black church. I was so happy that they would let me come and be with them and not hold my color against me.

"On the way up there, I worked for two hours preparing a speech for them. It was to have been a great speech and I was bursting at the seams to tell them all about it, and then an amazing thing happened to me. (I had written down the entire speech in my notebook as I wanted to stay on the subject and not wander.) However, as I stood in the pulpit for moment trying to size up the congregation, you know what I saw? I saw Jesus take my speech and tear it into tiny little bits, little pieces, and throw them away and then he said, 'Mary, you were called to witness not to preach. Look fully into my face and tell them what you see.'"

"Wouldn't that be a good text for most preachers? Look fully into my face and tell them what you see. And the message that day just spoke itself without any notes or any effort on my part and when I finished, one of the most touching things happened that I shall never forget. One of the sisters came up and kissed me on the cheek and it was so tender and so moving, I thought I would never want to wash that cheek again lest I destroy the beauty of such a blessing. Oh, Brother Stanley, at that moment there wasn't any question of color or race. It was just one child of God loving another and meaning it, and it came to me that this is the perfect solution to the so-called race problem, being one in Him. They loved me as much as I did them and I never in my life felt His spirit more than when I was witnessing to them, for they were so responsive and we were like one spirit in Him. What a blessing and joy it is to be Christians."

Now I come to the real thing. These other excerpts have been preliminary. I believe I read this letter to you last year. It came to me during the Ashram and I read it to some of you. In the 45 years that I have travelled across the world and looked into the face of human need, into the heart of human need, I've received many letters. I've never received one quite like this. Written with simplicity but in power and it has blessed multitudes already and it has blessed me.

It was written two weeks after the tragic car accident where Mary's husband Roy was killed and it was a personal letter describing what had happened in the accident and what had happened inside Mary. I will begin with Mary's words. "At present I'm in the hospital with my youngest son Claude. I've been in the Kewanee hospital for a week and the doctor, a neurosurgeon, needs to operate on Claude. Claude has a bad skull fracture and it's not looking too good."

"Teddy has been released from hospital. They can't operate on Claude until Tuesday morning at the earliest. His head is still so swollen and if he were older the doctor would drain it before surgery, but little Claude has been through so much already they don't want to hurt him anymore. His legs began to get stiff yesterday and he can't turn himself over without a great deal of pain. They're watching him closely. If he can make it through to Easter, that would be a good sign."

"How grateful I am that God healed my wounds enough so that I now have the strength to stay with him. My hand has a few fractures as do the ribs on my left side but my leg wasn't broken, nor my jaw as they first thought. I'm still very sore and bruised all over but otherwise just fine. I'm trying hard with grace from God not to worry over Claude's condition but to just trust and keep my mind free so I can be able to help him all I can. He really needs a strong mother now and I know God will help me be strong for God has already done miracles for me."

"Brother Stanley, ever since a year ago at the Ashram in Texas during the silent communion service, I've understood what death really is, and I've tried to tell others about just how beautiful an experience it would really be. It seemed to me at that communion service, that I really caught a glimpse into eternity and it's so beautiful that my heart nearly broke with joy and rapture. Well, it is one thing to tell someone something and another thing to go through it yourself, and so I wondered if when my time came to experience death, if it would hit me as an evil thing or if it would still seem to be the beautiful thing it was to me last year. Now I can tell you with all truthfulness that my original opinion has only been strengthened."

"I can honestly say Brother Stanley that at least for me, death doesn't have any sting. This may seem strange to you as it certainly is to so many others, especially the doctors and nurses. However, even when they told me that Roy was killed, I just couldn't feel one bit like crying. I haven't shed a tear over it nor do I feel like crying. God has been teaching me so much these last 15 months and he has so transformed my thinking that now I see this accident in its true light and not as a personal issue at all. You must agree that that viewpoint is a miracle."

"The truck that caused the accident passed another car and when he saw us coming toward him, the driver applied his brakes to slow down and get back into his lane, but the wheels of his truck locked and threw his truck sideways in front of our car and we hit him head on. The driver of the truck was utterly helpless and it was really just an accident. Roy didn't suffer at all as he was killed instantly."

"It is not tragic just because it happened to me. I know that when two cars going 45 or 50 miles per hour hit head-on, it is inevitable that someone gets badly hurt or killed. We just happened to be in the path of the truck. I certainly do know that it's not God's will that we got hurt or that Roy was killed. However, since God made us human, he also made us free and so we have the power to help or hurt one another. The laws of the universe are truly dependable laws; they work the same no matter who uses them or breaks them and how grateful I am that this is so."

"God was right there the night of the accident. I saw him in the faces of those who wanted to help us out of the compassion in their hearts. I saw God in the face of the ambulance driver who was so grieved when he saw it was his friends in the accident that he could hardly speak. I saw God in the faces of the doctors who instantly came to help us and worked for hours sewing us up and making us comfortable and then again in the faces of the 400 family and friends who came to Roy's funeral. Brother Loyal was at my bedside almost as soon as humanly possible. God was present in the flowers and cards of sympathy, from people from all over. And most of all God was present in that still small voice that said over and over again to me, 'Be not afraid, for lo I am with you always even unto the end of the world.' And then God said, 'I'm the resurrection and the life, and whosoever believeth in me, though he were dead yet shall he live and whosoever liveth and believeth in me shall never die. Believest thou this?' and I said, 'Yes, my precious Lord. I do believe that you are the one true God of the living,' and from then on my soul has been completely free of all anxiety and fear. All this was made possible by His holy love."

"God has been so close to me every moment that I feel really as if I had the wings of an eagle, (or an angel) and my heart is singing at the top of its voice our Ashram song *'I will not be afraid.'* It is the 1951 miracle that my dear precious Jesus performed in me, for while I thought it possible for me to accept death, little did I dream I could rejoice and sing in very face of it. But you know it was not me but Jesus in me who made that possible. All He has ever asked was that I stay open, just stay open and He has poured his blessings into me. Life looks just as beautiful today to me as it did two weeks ago because I really discovered something wonderful, that if you really do keep your eyes upon Jesus, you can go through any storm life has, and not have your spiritual equilibrium upset."

"But looking at Jesus and not at yourself is the most significant thing. At the Green Lake Ashram's prayer room Bible I found this verse, 'Mary has chosen that good part that should not be taken from her,' and those same words tell me now that I've chosen that good part of my husband that no one can ever take that away from me. He is one with me now in the spirit of our Lord. It is as if he had just gone upstairs to rest and I will go too when I finish what I'm doing, and we shall see each other again in the morning. So please my dear brother do not pity me for I find it impossible to pity myself, but feel extremely grateful to our precious Lord for standing by me, He really has."

"Your prayers were certainly felt but never have I felt the presence of God so strongly as in this past week. I'm sorry you had to hear all the news of the car accident and

Roy's death at the Ashram." (We received the news of it at the Kerrville Ashram.) "I knew you would want to know, but rest assured that your many prayers were answered, and my faith in God is twice what it was. I feel even relaxed about Claude and know that since he is God's child, God is even more interested in his welfare than I am and everything will be fine."

She then writes what happened just before her son's brain surgery and I will add this section. "After Claude went to sleep the night before his operation, I went to the window and I had a talk with God about the whole situation. I told Him that I could not ask Him to save Claude for me; but that he was His little boy too and for Him to just be with him all through the operation and that I wasn't going to worry about it as God had more at stake in the matter than I did."

But looking at Jesus and not at yourself is the most significant thing.

"It was very hard for me to tell God that as I had a real battle going on inside of me even at that moment. You see half of me was saying 'Tell God to save your little son, if He loves you,' and the other half was saying, 'Thou shall not tempt the Lord thy God. Trust in Him. Do not tell Him what to do. He did not even save His own son because he loved you so much and you would now ask Him to save your son? Pray for grace and strength to bear the outcome whichever way it falls and trust your Father with all your heart and mind and soul.'"

"Of course the last guidance is what I listened to, and finally my heart said, 'Dear Lord I trust and believe and I love you. Amen,' and at that moment I felt a great peace come down on me greater than ever before, as if a great weight had been lifted from my shoulders, and I slept a heavenly sleep all night long. In the morning I was happy and singing and even wheeled Claude to the operating room. I said goodbye to him with a smile. He smiled back and said, 'See you soon, Mommy.' When the surgeon saw me with a peaceful but radiant face, he said 'I've seen everything now and everything will be all right.' It was all right. The boy is well."

"All the hospital's doctors and nurses were talking about what happened to me. They said that they had never seen anyone look death right in the face and not bat an eye. When I told them just what God had done for me and what I thought death was, they said they felt so much better for they'd always feared it, not understanding it, and they were certain I was telling the truth because my reaction spoke for itself. They thought that they would even like to start going to church again. I tell you all this so you can see how when God enters the picture, glory breaks out all around. Thank you for all you've done for me. I can never thank you enough for all your prayers on my behalf."

"The hardest part was telling Teddy about his daddy. It was as if I ran a long sharp dagger right down into his little heart but God will heal the wound and he took the information like a soldier. I have still to tell Claude when he is well again. God bless you and keep you. Let me know whenever you are in Illinois and if possible, I'll try to see you. In Christ, your happy sister, Mary."

One would have thought that Mary's experience right after the accident could have been a spurt of positive energy but then she would lose that feeling over time and

272

become depressed or angry. However, it's been a year since the accident happened. She has never become depressed or angry. As far as one can see, she has not had the slightest reaction of sorrow or self-pity or a glance backward.

Mary was in the Kerrville Ashram recently and while she was there, it was a year to the day of the accident; Mary went into the prayer room on that anniversary day and stayed for three hours. When she came out she said, "Brother Stanley, did you ever sit down for three hours and say just two words? I've been sitting in the prayer room for three hours just saying two words; thank you, thank you, thank you." It shows how profound and yet simple Christianity can be when we really accept it and take it with all our heart.

Now God has no favorites. What God's is doing for Mary Webster he'll do for any of us, provided we come with simplicity and singleness of heart, and pay the price of surrender and obedience.

Now God has no favorites. What God's is doing for Mary Webster he'll do for any of us, provided we come with simplicity and singleness of heart, and pay the price of surrender and obedience. Whatever happens to Mary Webster in the future, if she walks softly with God, then she's going far and whatever happens, she's spreading glory everywhere she goes. I saw her speak at the Kerrville Ashram vespers and I have never seen an audience hang on to every word that she uttered. The words were simple and direct.I witnessed the group listening to her in the grip of the spirit of God, for the spirit of God had hold of a simple, trusting, obedient life.

This all means then that the latchstring to the Kingdom of God is open to every one of us and you can have all that you want. There's no favoritism here. It's open to everybody. I'm laying the tribute of my love and gratitude for her at Christ's feet, her Christ, my Christ and yours. Other people have met tragedy too and have met it wonderfully, but I've never quite seen anyone go through such a thing on wings and stay on wings. It's wonderful to be a Christian.

Shall we pray?

In the quietness of this moment, let's take that last lingering thing and lay it at His feet. That last bit of self-pity, resentment, fear, self-centeredness and lay it at His feet. Take God's forgiveness and go forward rejoicing. Dear Father, dismiss us with Thy blessing and may we go out of here belonging to Thee, no strings attached, nothing held back. May I suggest that some of us go to the prayer chapel, some go to the vespers at Hillside Chapel, but let's all settle all matters with God tonight, and come back in the morning changed. And now brothers and sisters we commend you to God, and to the word of His grace, which is able to build you up and give you an inheritance among them who are sanctified. Amen.

Mary Webster, E. Stanley Jones and others, Japan 1959

Mary Webster, E. Stanley Jones and others, Japan 1971

AFTERWORD

THE STORY OF MARY WEBSTER is a profound example of the power of a laywoman to become a center of evangelistic spiritual power. Jones met Mary Webster in the 1950s and found her to be a perfect example of how an ordinary life transformed and redeemed could become a force for sharing the love of Jesus Christ with all she encountered.

I believe that Mary was often surprised by the extent of her transformation. She knew very well where she had come from and the nature of her character before Jesus entered her life. Her very considerable humility often led her to believe that she did not bring much to evangelism efforts. However, to those who knew Mary, she brought her full self to her efforts to share Jesus. She had remarkable storytelling gifts and the capacity to make complex theology understandable through her personal illustrations. I hope that the reader has been inspired by the possibilities that are available to each of us when we fully surrender our lives to Christ and like Mary, keep our eyes on Jesus.

Mary Webster in c.1998

ABOUT THE COMPILER

DR. ANNE MATHEWS-YOUNES is a psychologist who currently works for the U.S. Federal Government. In 1980, she completed her doctorate in Counseling and Consulting Psychology from Harvard University and has worked in state and federal mental health agencies for the past 36 years in programs designed to prevent school violence and suicide, promote mental health and prevent mental and behavioral disorders, treat child trauma, and support disaster, terrorism and bioterrorism preparedness and response.

Dr. Mathews-Younes has also completed a Master's Degree in Theological Studies at Wesley Theological Seminary in Washington, D.C., as well as a Doctoral Degree in Ministry from that same seminary. Both of her theology degree theses focused on the life, mission and theology of her late grandfather, E. Stanley Jones, with whom she traveled extensively through India and Africa.

Dr. Mathews-Younes is the President of the E. Stanley Jones Foundation (www.estanley-jonesfoundation.com) which is dedicated to preserving and extending the legacy of the late E. Stanley Jones who blessed millions of people around the world with his preaching, teaching and prolific spiritual writings. She has also served as the Vice-President of the United Christian Ashrams Board, a spiritual retreat organization founded by E. Stanley Jones. Her book, *Living Upon the Way: Selected Sermons of E. Stanley Jones on Surrender*, was published in 2008.

Anne can be reached at:
Email: anne@estanleyjonesfoundation.com

Anne Mathews-Younes and E. Stanley Jones, India, 1967

ABOUT
THE E. STANLEY JONES
FOUNDATION

The E. Stanley Jones Foundation is dedicated to bold and fruitful evangelism which shares the life-changing message of Jesus Christ to persons of all ages, backgrounds, life situations and locations. The Foundation is also dedicated to preserving and extending the legacy of the late E. Stanley Jones who blessed millions of people around the world with his preaching, teaching and prolific written words proclaiming Jesus is Lord! Our vision is to reach every generation with the message of Jesus Christ; enlighten spiritual growth through education and inspiration; prepare both Christian leaders and laity to be followers of Jesus Christ, and make known the Kingdom of God today.

For more information and our current

programs, kindly visit us at:

www.estanleyjonesfoundation.com

Thank you!

OTHER PUBLICATIONS
of the E. Stanley Jones Foundation

Order your copies from *Amazon.com, CreateSpace.com* and
The E. Stanley Jones Foundation

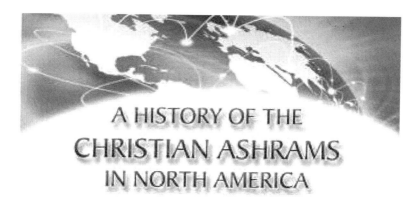

A HISTORY OF THE
CHRISTIAN ASHRAMS
IN NORTH AMERICA

COMPILED AND EDITED BY

Anne Mathews-Younes

Order your copies from *Amazon.com, CreateSpace.com* and
The E. Stanley Jones Foundation

Coming Soon

Is The Kingdom of God Realism?
by E. Stanley Jones

and more!

75284739R00158

Made in the USA
Columbia, SC
21 August 2017